THE *Sisters Rosensweig*

WENDY WASSERSTEIN

THE *Sisters Rosensweig*

Harcourt Brace & Company

New York   San Diego   London

Library of Congress Cataloging-in-Publication Data
Wasserstein, Wendy.
The sisters Rosensweig/Wendy Wasserstein. — 1st ed.
p.   cm.
ISBN 0-15-182692-7
1. Sisters — England — London — Drama.   I. Title.
PS3573.A798S5   1993
812'.54 — dc20   93-224

Designed by Camilla Filancia
Printed in the United States of America
First edition   A B C D E

For Sandra

PREFACE

I sat through the first preview of this play on September 25, 1992 beside André Bishop, my old friend and the artistic director of Lincoln Center Theater, in a semi state of shock. To my mind *The Sisters Rosensweig* was my most serious effort—a one-set, non-episodic play, complete with unities of time, place, and action, deliberately set on the eve of a momentous historical event, and even with the pretense of echoing those three far more famous stage sisters who yearned for Moscow.

But just five minutes into the first act the audience was rapidly chuckling, and by the time Dr. Gorgeous entered in her shocking pink fake Chanel suit and vinylette Louis Vuitton luggage, they were convulsed with laughter. André tapped my shoulder. "Wendy, what is happening here? I've never seen anything like this."

I thought to myself, well, I'm glad the subscribers are happy, but my evaluation of my own work is clearly askew. No wonder it took forever to title this play. (Former attempts were *The Sisters Gorgeous, The Concert of Europe,* and *Sara, Pfeni, and Gorgeous.*) That night I felt that if I thought I wrote *Medea*, it would probably in reality resemble the old television show *Queen for a Day*.

Interestingly, however, as that first preview moved into the darker scenes of the second act, the audience grew restless. After the show, when Daniel Sullivan, the director, and I walked to a cast party, he said to me, "Now the hard part begins. Now we have to find the balance."

Dan has an unerring ability to put his finger always on the heart of the matter. This is neither a serious nor a comedic play. It is hopefully both. The trick in writing it, playing it, or even reading it, is to find the balance between the bright colors of humor and the serious issues of identity, self-loathing, and the possibility for intimacy and love when it seems no longer possible or, sadder yet, no longer necessary.

I don't think a play is really playing if the author has to explain it. Did Chekhov have three sisters? Did George S. Kaufman and Moss Hart want to take it with them? And did Noel Coward have a design for living? I leave such questions to guest deconstructionists on obscure late-night talk shows. All I can say is that *The Sisters Rosensweig* and I owe much to all four playwrights.

For the record, I am the youngest of three sisters, and my oldest sister never dated a faux furrier. However, I have known many actresses whose career opportunities diminished because they made the grievous error of growing older. Therefore I deliberately set out to write smart and funny parts for women over forty. I also created, hopefully, a very nice man who falls in love at first sight with one of them. This is not an angry play. It is one of possibilities. My first playwriting teacher told me there is order in art, not in life. My contention is that life can imitate art if the artist changes the accepted variables. Mervyn, the world leader in synthetic animal protective covering, and Sara, the international banker, are not romantic fantasies. They are grownups whom we don't get to see on stage often enough.

One issue that hasn't been addressed much about *The Sisters Rosensweig* is that of identity. Geoffrey, the world-class director and one of my favorite people in this play, confesses to his beloved Pfeni, "You don't know what it's like to have absolutely no idea who you are!" Despite their maturity, most of the characters in the play are struggling with who they are. There's a reason why these three sisters are from Brooklyn and the play takes place in Queen Anne's Gate, London.

Plays, even in published form, are a collaboration. This one owes its transformation from page to life and back again to Daniel Sullivan. I know that Dan considers *The Sisters Rosensweig* the third in his Jewish themes trilogy: previous to this play he directed consecutively *Conversations with My Father* by Herb Gardner and *The Substance of Fire* by Jon Robin Baitz. Maybe Dan is the theatrical Messiah. Not a bad job for an Irishman from Seattle.

This play also marks a trilogy for André Bishop and me. He produced my last two plays, *The Heidi Chronicles* and *Isn't It Romantic* at Playwrights Horizons, and this is our first effort together at Lincoln Center. Often I've been asked what exactly is André's great gift with new American plays. André always seems to know when to impose his opinion and when to let go. And when he does speak, it's never really an imposition, because, and this is an embarrassing truth, he's always right.

Thanks are also due to Daniel Swee for his casting couch, to Anne Cattaneo for her whips-and-bondage dramaturgy, and to Roy Harris, our stage manager, who from the very first reading had a crush on all the sisters Rosensweig. The ladies were also nurtured through the consistently generous friendship of Caroline Aaron, Christopher Durang, William Finn, Michiko Kakutani, Peter Parnell, and Paul Rudnick.

When I first finished this play, I had no idea how any character would get on or off the stage much less go upstairs or down. Moreover, I included elaborate descriptions for clothes for Dr. Gorgeous which I had no idea existed, for instance, "She enters in a fake Ungaro cocktail dress." (I wouldn't recognize a real Ungaro even if I wore one.) In many ways, then, the real unities herein were created by John Lee Beatty, the set designer, and Jane Greenwood, the costume designer. Finally, the sisters Rosensweig themselves would not have existed if it hadn't been for the lighting designer, Pat Collins, who took me aside during a tech-rehearsal of *The Heidi Chronicles* in Los Angeles and told me to go home and write a play.

On a Sunday matinee a month after *The Sisters Rosensweig* opened, I went back to the Mitzi Newhouse Theatre to see the play. It was the first time I wasn't hiding in the light booth, or taking preview notes in the anonymity of the last row. As I watched it, I became, frankly, a little envious of the author. Whoever wrote this play lucked out with a spectacular cast. Clearly, the success of the evening was due in large part to the author's having been in a rehearsal room with every single one of them.

At the end of the evening, when I saw the audience no longer restless, but actually weeping, I thought to myself that this author must be very mature. She must believe in family and personal history. She must believe in the challenge and tradition of well-structured plays. She must believe there are possibilities. Obviously, then, the author could not possibly be me.   WENDY WASSERSTEIN
New York, December 1992

The Sisters Rosensweig was first performed, in an earlier version, in the Seattle Repertory Theatre New Plays Reading Series, April 1992.

The play opened October 22, 1992 at Lincoln Center Theater at the Mitzi E. Newhouse. It was directed by Daniel Sullivan; the sets were designed by John Lee Beatty; costumes by Jane Greenwood; lighting by Pat Collins; sound by Guy Sherman/Aural Fixation. Roy Harris was production stage manager; Jeff Hamlin was production manager. The cast was as follows, in order of appearance:

TESS GOODE	Julie Dretzin
PFENI ROSENSWEIG	Frances McDormand
SARA GOODE	Jane Alexander
GEOFFREY DUNCAN	John Vickery
MERVYN KANT	Robert Klein
GORGEOUS TEITELBAUM	Madeline Kahn
TOM VALIUNUS	Patrick Fitzgerald
NICHOLAS PYM	Rex Robbins

The play moves to Broadway, to the Barrymore Theatre, March 1993. The cast remains the same, except that Christine Estabrook replaces Frances McDormand in the role of Pfeni Rosensweig.

THE *Sisters*
Rosensweig

A CT O NE

A weekend in late August, 1991.

A sitting room in Queen Anne's Gate, London.

S CENE 1

Late morning Friday. The room is decorator "done" with cozy, comfy, but expensive chintz couches, chairs, and window treatments. There is a dining room upstage right and a staircase upstage left leading to the bedrooms. TESS, *seventeen, in blue jeans and a flannel shirt, is listening to* SARA's *collegiate all-women's singing group doing an a cappella version of "Shine On Harvest Moon." She speaks into a tape recorder.*

TESS: Elongated note on moon. A harvest moon is a full September moon. *The doorbell rings.* Also notice the use of the vernacular, "I ain't had no lovin'."

The doorbell rings.

SARA, *offstage:* Tessie, get the door! *The doorbell rings.*

TESS *lowers the music and races towards the door. Her aunt,* PFENI, *forty, enters. She carries at least five shopping bags brimming with clothes, gifts, and a laptop computer.* PFENI

appears younger than her age, and wears comfortable pants
and jacket, well known to journalists and world travelers.

PFENI: His name was Jesse.
TESS: Aunt Pfeni!
PFENI: Jesse the Sikh.
TESS: We've been waiting for you. Mother and I had no idea
what time you'd be coming.
PFENI: Blame it all on Jesse. Jesse the Sikh.
TESS: Who?
PFENI: That was the name of my taxi driver. He was a Sikh.
The lion of India.
TESS: My mother says you exaggerate.
PFENI: He drove me all last night around Bombay until all I
could catch was the last plane.
TESS: Well, my mother's going to be delighted you actually
showed up.
PFENI: And you, are you delighted? *They embrace. The mu-*
sic has changed to the all-women's version of "Begin the
Beguine." They begin dancing. What are you listening
to?
TESS: My mother's college singing group. This was their signature song. We're doing biographies of our parents' early
years for our school summer project. It's pretentious. *Shuts*
off the music. I can't wait to leave London and go back
home to school.
PFENI: Did your mother say you could?
TESS: Are you kidding? The woman who named me for Tess
of the D'Urbervilles? The only American who is convinced that Harvard and Yale are second-rate institutions. She won't even discuss it.

"Well, my mother's going to be delighted you actually showed up."
(Julie Dretzin, Francis McDormand) ©1992 Martha Swope

SARA *enters from upstairs. She is a very handsome woman
of fifty-four. Even in the bathrobe she's now wearing, she
exudes dignity and authority.*

SARA: Tess, who are you talking to? Hello my baby sister! I
didn't know you were here. *Kisses her on the cheek.*
Tessie, I never said Harvard and Yale were second-rate
institutions. I said they were floundering on their way to
being second rate.

PFENI: It's good to see you, Sara.

SARA: Did you sleep at all on the plane? I was just reading
a very good piece in *The Financial Times* about the Rus-
sian coup by that friend of yours who won the Overseas
Press Award this year. Isn't it time you won that?

PFENI: Tessie, come here and protect me from your mother.

TESS: My English teacher at Westminster assigned Aunt Pfeni's
book for next semester.

SARA Really? Which one?

TESS: *Life in the Afghan Village.* It's for our women's seg-
ment. She says when Aunt Pfeni began using her exper-
tise to write travel columns, she became counterrevolutionary.

PFENI: Did she tell you who my dentist is?

SARA: Pfeni's books are super. Brilliant. Having a separate
category for women's writing is counterrevolutionary.

TESS: Well, it doesn't matter anyway. I'm going to study
hairdressing so I can make my way in the world.

SARA: Tessie, my luv, if you want to be a hairdresser, I'll
still love you and be very proud of you. Of course the
way the economy is going, you'd be far more practical
choosing a less luxury-oriented field.

PFENI: Tessie, have you considered welding?

SARA: Pfeni, you're diverting the argument.

PFENI, *with an accent:* Vell excuse me for living.

SARA: We're discussing Tessie's future! *The phone rings.* Yes, hello. Oh, hello Nick! How nice to hear from you.

TESS, *rolling her eyes:* Oh, God, it's him!

SARA: Could you hold while I take this in the kitchen? Pfeni, please share with Tessie your worldly advice. *Exits.*

TESS: My mother says she worries about me because I'm so much like you. She says you compulsively travel because you have a fear of commitment, and when you do stay in one place, you become emotional and defensive just like me.

PFENI: Tessie, honey, I'm so sorry. I didn't know it was contagious. *Begins rummaging through her shopping bags.* There's a valuable gift for you in one of these.

TESS: Aunt Pfeni, why don't you have any suitcases?

PFENI: Because your grandmother Rita told me that only crazy people travel with shopping bags. So I've made it my personal signature ever since. *Hands a package to* TESS. *It contains a statue of Shiva.* Here it is. This god will destroy all evil and bring you hope, rebirth, and a life-time guarantee that under no circumstances will you grow up to be like me.

TESS: Why does it have so many arms?

PFENI: It's very versatile. Its name is Shiva the destroyer. I found it on Elephanta Island off the coast of Bombay yesterday. A hot tip for where to shop in the Indian Ocean.

TESS: Aunt Pfeni?

PFENI: Niece Tess?

TESS: Can I give this to my mother? My mother's in desperate need of hope and rebirth. I think she's perfectly content to relive her life through me.

SARA *reenters.*

SARA: Good news. Nick Pym's coming to dinner tonight.

TESS: You know, mother, there are homeless people sleeping under Charing Cross Station.

SARA: Do you think Nick Pym would prefer to have my birthday dinner with them?

TESS: Mother, I just don't think it's right to have bourgeois dinner parties with capitalists like Nicholas Pym when people are living in boxes under Charing Cross Station.

SARA, *staring at* TESS: Pfeni, hasn't Tess grown up brilliantly.

TESS: Mother, now you're the one diverting the argument!

SARA: I don't know how it happened, but I've been blessed with a totally beautiful and brilliant daughter. My daughter just happens to be perfect. I tell your Aunt Pfeni to be certain that sometime during her peripatetic life she have at least one child, because the greatest joy of my life is having you.

TESS: Mother, that's sentimental revisionist history! Hermia Cox-Jones's father says you have the biggest balls at the Hong Kong/Shanghai Bank worldwide.

PFENI: Pish-pish.

SARA: Pfeni, there's something very New York about your tone today.

PFENI: Vell, excuse me for living two times.

TESS: What do you mean, New York?

SARA: Well . . .

PFENI: Tessie, many decades and a continent ago, when your mother was a freshman at Radcliffe and I was still living home with your grandparents in Flatbush, Brooklyn, a very nice man named Harry Rose called our house every morning. Mr. Rose was the head salesman at Grampa's Kiddie Tog factory.

SARA: What is your point, Pfeni?

PFENI: Tessie, Mr. Rose liked to catch Grampa to discuss the day's business just when the entire house would be waking up. So every day at seven A.M. I'd rush to pick up the phone just to hear Mr. Rose say, "Hallo, Maury, is that you?" And then I'd answer, "No, Mr. Rose. It's me. Maury's daughter Penny." And he'd always say, "Vell, excuse me for living, Penny, but how could you recognize it was me?"

TESS: So Mr. Harry Rose was New York?

SARA: New York in a way that has very little to do with us. Pfeni's the one who's guilty of revisionist history, my luv. Pfeni's the one who's romanticized a world we never belonged to.

PFENI: I was mistaken. Mr. Rose never called our house every morning. It was Louis Auchincloss.

SARA: You see, Tessie. I told you Pfeni's defensive just like you.

TESS: You have no sense of humor, mother, none.

SARA, *with an accent:* What? You think you're telling me something I don't know. *Smiles.* That was very New York.

TESS: I gotta go. I'm meeting Tom. Can he come to this late dinner too?

PFENI: Who's Tom?

SARA: Who's Tom, Tessie?

TESS: Tom Valiunus is the man I'm currently seeing.

SARA: Tell Pfeni more. She's very good about people.

TESS: Tom's father owns a radio supply store in Liverpool, and he's hoping to go into the business if the economy turns around.

PFENI: That sounds nice.

TESS: Mother doesn't think so.

SARA: I never said that. I just don't know what you have in common with someone who dreams of selling radio parts. And you certainly don't have to chase him through greater Latvia.

TESS: Lithuania. Aunt Pfeni, Tom and I are very committed to the Lithuanian resistance. And because of the coup Tom feels we should be there.

PFENI: Vilnius was once the Jerusalem of Lithuania.

SARA: You're not being very helpful, Pfeni.

PFENI: There's also a good restaurant, the famous and traditional Old Cellar. Also, for plays, check out the Central Theatre of Vilnius.

SARA: That way, Tessie, when they send the tanks in, you and Tom can take in a quick hamburger and a show.

TESS: Mother, that's not funny.

SARA: I know. I have no sense of humor.

TESS: Aunt Pfeni, would you like to join Tom and me for tea today?

SARA: Aunt Pfeni, don't you think it's just slightly irregular for a nice Jewish girl from Connecticut to find her calling in the Lithuanian resistance?

TESS: But I'm not a nice Jewish girl from Connecticut. I'm an expatriate American who's lived in London for five years and the daughter of an atheist.

SARA: This has nothing to do with organized religion.

TESS: Mother, Tom comes from a perfectly balanced and normal family, which is something you've never managed to maintain despite being on the cover of *Fortune* twice. But if you like, I'll tell him that he's not invited to dinner here tonight with the socially acceptable, racist, sexist, and more than likely anti-Semitic Nicholas Pym.

SARA, *quietly:* Tessie, please invite Tom to supper tonight.

TESS, *kissing* SARA *on the cheek:* Tea is at Fortnum's at five.

SARA: Guess who's paying for the tea. I never met a freedom fighter who didn't enjoy a good meal. Pfeni, you must talk to her.

PFENI: I did talk to her.

SARA: She's determined to make her life the opposite of mine.

PFENI: That's exactly what we set out to do because of our mother.

SARA: Yes, but we were right.

PFENI: So, maybe, is Tessie. SARA *starts to move the shopping bags.* Sara, relax. I'll take them down later.

SARA, *picks up the Shiva:* I don't know why Tessie insists on bringing home junk like this from Portobello Road.

PFENI: I brought it from Bombay.

SARA: Oh, it's lovely.

PFENI *gives her the Shiva:* This will destroy all evil and bring you hope and rebirth.

SARA: I'm too old.

PFENI: You're not too old.

SARA: You don't know. You're only forty.

PFENI: Forty is old.

SARA: Oh, Pfeni, I'm so glad you're here.

PFENI: Did you think I'd let Dr. Gorgeous show up for your birthday and not be here?

SARA: Your sister's not just showing up for my birthday. She's leading the Temple Beth El sisterhood on a tour of the crown jewels.

PFENI: But she managed to plan it in time for your birthday.

SARA: True. You're a good sister, Pfeni Rosensweig. Pfeni! God, what an awful name! Why do you keep it? *Sits with* PFENI *on the couch. Puts her feet up on* PFENI.

PFENI: Penny Rosensweig wasn't any better. Now, Sara Goode, on the other hand, is a great name.

SARA: Multiple divorce is a brilliant thing. You get so many names to choose from. But my second was definitely my best. And how nice that there is now a Mrs. Samantha Goode, Mrs. Melissa Goode, Mrs. Pamela Goode, and, as of last year, the twenty-four-year-old Mrs. Sushiro Goode. We could form the Wives of Kenneth Goode Club, with branches in Chicago, New York, London, and Tokyo. Well, never mind. I'm looking forward to us growing old together. Like two old-maid spinsters in a Muriel Spark novel.

PFENI: Sara, that's beyond depressing.

SARA: No it isn't. It could be rather cozy. You could stop traveling, finally settle into the downstairs flat, and grow more and more eccentric, and I could get meaner and crabbier.

PFENI: But I have Geoffrey.

SARA: Well, he can visit us. He's here all the time anyway.

PFENI: Geoffrey says we'll live together when his house is finished.

SARA: That man has no intention of ever living there, when he can enjoy the hospitality of all his friends.

PFENI: Geoffrey adds a little texture to your life.

SARA: I don't need that much texture in my life. You'd be better off getting old with me. Is Geoffrey joining us for dinner tonight?

PFENI: I hope so.

SARA *gets up from the couch:* Good. Maybe he'll solve both our problems and fall madly in love with Tom and lead him on the children's crusade to Vilnius. *Pause.* Indulge me, Pfeni. I told you, I'm an old and bitter woman.

PFENI: You're not old and bitter. You're anticipating an era of hope and rebirth.

SARA: Promise me you'll stay awhile this time. The other night I was singing in the kitchen and Tessie told me to stop. She hates it when I sing now. She says I'm too grown-up and scary to sing. Am I very scary?

PFENI: Terrifying. But what about her summer project? She was listening to your college group when I came in.

SARA: Her thesis is to prove that my early years have no bearing on my present life. Frankly, I can hardly remember my early years. You know what I was thinking about the other night? What happens to the Cannibal King after Ah-rump Da-de-ya-de-day.

PFENI: Sara, you're speaking in tongues.

SARA: The Cannibal King with the big nose ring.

PFENI: Oh, *that* Cannibal King with the big nose ring! *Begins to sing:*

> Fell in love with the dusky maid,
> And every night in the pale moonlight
> This is what she'd say . . .

SARA *and* PFENI *begin to play patty-cake.*

SARA & PFENI, *spoken:*

> Ah-rump, Ah-rump, Ah-rump, Da-de-ya-de-day,
> Ah-rump, Ah-rump, Ah-rump, Da-de-ya-de-day.

SARA: Now what?

PFENI *begins to sing quickly:*

Let's build a bungalow big enough for two,
Big enough for two, my honey . . .

SARA: Pfeni, that's it. That's it. You're a genius!
PFENI:

Big enough for two,
Big enough for two,
And when we're married, happy we'll be,
Under the bamboo,
Under the bamboo tree.

SARA & PFENI, SARA *continue to play patty-cake as* PFENI
sings:

If you'll be M-I-N-E mine
I'll be T-H-I-N-E thine,
And I'll L-O-V-E love you
All the T-I-M-E time.

Let's take an L-A-R-K lark
Into the P-A-R-K park,
And I'll K-I-S-S kiss you
In the D-A-R-K dark.

You are the B-E-S-T best
Of all the R-E-S-T rest,
And I'll L-O-V-E love you
All the T-I-M-E time.

GEOFFREY, *an attractive forty-year-old man in a hip leather
jacket and a Sunset in Penang T-shirt, enters the house. He*

carries an overnight bag and immediately begins applauding.

GEOFFREY: That was brilliant! Just brilliant! But you must make the recitative even faster, even crisper.

PFENI *waves at him:* Hello, Geoffrey.

GEOFFREY: Hello my luv. And ready, "You are the B-E-S-T best of all the R-E-S-T rest." And one, two, three . . . *Conducts them.*

SARA & PFENI, *very quickly:*

> You are the B-E-S-T best
> Of all the R-E-S-T rest,
> And I'll L-O-V-E love you
> All the T-I-M-E time.

GEOFFREY, *applauding:* Bravo! Bravo! Bravo the sisters Rosensweig! *Lifts up* PFENI *and carries her to the downstairs exit.*

SARA *remains on stage looking distractedly out the window.*

S C E N E 2

Later that afternoon. PFENI *enters from her apartment, which is downstairs.* GEOFFREY *follows her.*

GEOFFREY: The problem with you, Pfeni darling, is that you just don't like women very much.

PFENI: That's not true.

GEOFFREY: Of course it is, luv. Think about it. Women make you feel competitive and insecure.

PFENI: That's nonsense, Geoffrey.

GEOFFREY: It's all right, darling. You can't like everyone.

PFENI: And I suppose that you, on the other hand, are open to people of all sexes, race, and color.

GEOFFREY *starts to sing:* "I am everyday people!" Sly and the Family Stone, 1969.

PFENI: Sara says we should stop seeing each other. She says she and I should grow old together.

GEOFFREY: Pfeni my luv, all you've talked about since you've arrived here is Sara. How guilty you feel that she was ill. How guilty you feel that she's alone. How much you love her. How much you can't bear to be around her.

How much you want her praise. How little you care for her opinions.

PFENI: That's not true.

GEOFFREY: All I know is that whenever you're around that woman, you tell me we have to stop seeing each other. My darling, we hardly ever do see each other. I'm always in rehearsal and you're in Timbuktu half the year. It's a bloody brilliant relationship. *Kisses her on the forehead.*

PFENI: Oh my God, my life is stuck. "I've forgotten the Italian for window."

GEOFFREY: Very good! *Three Sisters,* Act III. Now, Pfeni darling, see how worthwhile it's been knowing me. If not for me, you'd still think that *Uncle Vanya* was a Neil Simon play about his pathetic uncle in the Bronx.

PFENI: And now instead I've had a three-year relationship with an internationally renowned director and bisexual.

GEOFFREY: You left out botanist. I read botany at Cambridge. And I also put that "f" betwixt your name. If not for me, you'd be plain and simple Penny Rosensweig.

PFENI: Thank you. I have your "f" to keep me warm.

GEOFFREY: For Christ's sake, Pfeni, if you want to find unconditional love, have a baby. Adopt a red and fuzzy brood of them. Better yet, have artificial insemination. *Lifts up a water glass.* "Hello darling, this is Daddy. Say good morning to your daddy." "Morning, Daddy." Or you could become a lesbian. Most of the really interesting women I know are lesbians.

PFENI: Just tell me one thing? What do you still get out of this?

GEOFFREY: T-shirts from all over the world. Would I be

sporting Sunset in Penang if not for you? I've been meaning to ask you, darling, where is Penang?

PFENI: Malaysia. Somerset Maugham lived there.

GEOFFREY: This is what's so wonderful about dating a nice American Jewish girl! You're all so well versed in British colonial history. *Embraces her.* Pfeni, my luv, trust me. I am still very happy with you.

PFENI: You wouldn't like to meet a nice man?

GEOFFREY: I meet nice men all the time. I'm a director.

PFENI: I mean some nice man for you to come home to.

GEOFFREY: I've already done that, my darling, and he left me for Rum-Tum-Tugger.

PFENI: Who?

GEOFFREY: Jordan left me for that chorus boy from *Cats.*

PFENI: But that was ages ago.

GEOFFREY: Exactly. And then I met you at the ballet, and Jordan became England's hottest flatware designer. He's soon to be knighted "Sir Cutlery."

PFENI: But . . .

GEOFFREY: But what? Do you want to know if I have my eye on anyone in my show? Is it true what they say about *The Scarlet Pimpernel?* My darling, I am committed. I've signed exclusively with you. Have I told you I've been offered the animated *Fawlty Towers?* I could fit it in next season between *The Duchess of Malfi* and *Oklahoma!* On the other hand, my film career is nowhere near where it should be. Unfortunately, movies do mean enduring extended time in Los Angeles. Why don't you have your film capital somewhere more civilized, like *Des Moines? Pronounces it as if it were French.*

PFENI: Where?

GEOFFREY: *Des Moines,* Idaho.

PFENI: It's Des Moines. And it's in Iowa. I'll see what I can do.

GEOFFREY: Pfeni, my angel, I wish you knew what a gorgeous person you are.

PFENI: My sister is gorgeous. I'm not.

GEOFFREY: My darling, I can't waste any more time listening to your negativity and self-criticism. You're becoming almost as self-absorbed as I am. Besides, I'm expecting two hundred homeless people who live under Charing Cross Station to arrive here in just a few.

PFENI: To arrive here? At Sara's house?

GEOFFREY: Well, it's not all two hundred of them, actually. It's closer to a small delegation, and I told them to be certain to ring the downstairs bell and not Sara's.

PFENI: That was thoughtful!

GEOFFREY: Tell me what you think, my darling. I have an idea to do this year's homeless benefit at The National as a sort of story theatre. I want to hear their brilliant voices telling the simple human tale of their survival. The theatre's in danger of becoming hopelessly elitist. *The bell rings.* What's that? *The bell rings again.*

PFENI: The bell.

GEOFFREY: But that's not the downstairs bell.

PFENI: No.

GEOFFREY: What should we do?

PFENI: Let's invite your delegation to stay for Sara's birthday party.

The bell rings again.

GEOFFREY: I can't allow these people into Sara's house. They're desperate. They take things. They deserve to kill us for centuries of oppression.

PFENI: Relax. Go downstairs. I'll tell them to meet you down there.

GEOFFREY: Brilliant.

GEOFFREY *exits to the downstairs service entrance.* PFENI *answers the door.* MERV KANT, *a fifty-eight-year-old American in a wrinkled linen suit, stands in the door. He is immediately warm, but surprisingly sexy. He carries a Turnbull & Asser bag.*

MERV: Hi!

PFENI: Mr. Duncan said he'd prefer to meet you and your group downstairs. There's another entrance down the back.

MERV: My group? You mean my combo?

PFENI: You're not English.

MERV: No, and neither are you.

PFENI: Do you live under Charing Cross Station?

MERV: I live over Charing Cross Station, at the Savoy Hotel. May I leave this for Geoff? *Enters.*

PFENI: Who?

MERV: I like to call him Geoff. Drives him crazy. He tells me, "Murf, only someone who rhymes with surf can call me Geoff."

PFENI: Your name is "Murf the Surf"?

MERV: How do you do.

PFENI: Pfeni Rosensweig. I'll get him for you.

MERV: And tell him I went to the Turnbull sale and found the purple shirts we've been searching for. Honey, when I saw that shirt, I was kvelling—like I just discovered the double helix. PFENI, *knocking on the door:* Murf is here to say he just discovered the double helix.

GEOFFREY *comes out.*

MERV: Geoffrey, mazeltov, you've finally come out of the closet.

GEOFFREY: What ho, Sir Murf?

MERV: What ho! *Begins to sing and dance around the room.*

I found the shirt at Turnbull's-a-nanny-nanny-no.
I found the purple shirt at Turnbull's-a-nanny-nanny-no.
And I got one for you and I got one for me.

Gives GEOFFREY *the package.*

A-nanny-nanny-no.

MERV & GEOFFREY *sing and dance:*

I found the shirts at Turnbull's. A-nanny-nanny-no!

They finish in a big finale.

MERV, *to* PFENI: Honey, I would have gotten one for you, but I didn't know your size.

GEOFFREY: How did you find me here?

MERV: You left a message to meet you at seven.

GEOFFREY: But what about the homeless?

MERV: What about the homeless?

GEOFFREY: I believe I told them to meet me where I thought I'd be seeing you.

MERV: Where's that?

GEOFFREY: Drinks at the Savoy at seven. *Grabs his coat.*

Pfeni, offer Sir Murf a drink, and I'll try to head them off. *Kisses her.* Much love, angel. *Exits.*

MERV: So.

PFENI: So.

MERV: Would I like a drink?

PFENI: Would you?

MERV: Not really. Whose house am I in?

PFENI: My sister, Sara's.

MERV: It's very nice. What does her husband do?

PFENI: My sister is the managing director of the Hong Kong/ Shanghai Bank Europe.

MERV: Sounds like a smart girl.

PFENI: How did you meet Geoffrey?

MERV: Mutual friends. How did you meet Geoffrey?

PFENI: I sat next to him at *Giselle,* and he asked me to be the mother of his children.

SARA *enters, wearing an apron over pants and a sweater.*

SARA: Pfeni! Who's here? Hello.

MERV: Hi. Hello. Merv Kant.

PFENI: This is an American friend of Geoffrey's.

MERV: And you must be Pfeni's younger sister.

SARA: Ha ha ha. Are you here on holiday?

MERV: I was in Budapest last week with the American Jewish Congress.

SARA: Yes, well, Budapest seems to be quite popular recently.

MERV: And on Sunday we go to Ireland to have brunch with the Rabbi of Dublin.

SARA: Fascinating! Where's your friend Geoffrey?

MERV: He's stood me up for the homeless under Charing Cross Station.

SARA: Yes, they also seem to be quite popular these days.

PFENI: Well, I'd better go meet Tom and Tessie. Would you like to share a taxi, Merv?

MERV *looks at Sara:* No, I'm fine.

SARA: Pfeni, if you're only meeting Tessie now, when will you be home?

PFENI: Soon.

SARA: But you're already two hours late.

PFENI: Sara, doll, soon is soon. *With accent.* Now that was really New York! *Exits,* leaving the door wide open.

SARA *stands by the door, waiting for* MERV *to exit voluntarily.*

MERV: Your sister was just offering me a drink. Some cold water would be perfect. Thanks. SARA *goes to get him a drink.* So you and your sister are from New York!

SARA: My sister is a traveler, and I live right here in Queen Anne's Gate. Here's your water, Mr. Kant.

MERV: Thanks. Your sister tells me you're a brilliant woman.

SARA: I have a few opinions about European common currency. That hardly makes me brilliant.

MERV: Well, you're the first Jewish woman I've met to run a Hong Kong bank.

SARA: I'm the first woman to run a Hong Kong bank, Mr. Kant.

MERV: It used to be Kantlowitz. You're looking at your watch. Would you prefer that I leave?

SARA: I'm just wondering what time my daughter's coming home.

MERV: Relax. I had three children who never came home and they're all fine now. My oldest, Kip, is a semiotics professor at Boston University. That means he screens

Hiroshima, Mon Amour once a week. The other boy is a radiologist in North Carolina, Chapel Hill, and my baby, Eva, is a forest ranger in Israel. That means she works for the parks department in Haifa. And your daughter?

SARA: We're hoping she'll be up at Oxford next year.

MERV: She wants to stay here for school?

SARA: From what we've heard about the States now, I think it's wise.

MERV: Tell me what "we've heard."

SARA: It's conventional wisdom, really.

MERV: Really?

SARA: Well, obviously what you have is a society in transition. You've got an industrial economy that is rapidly being transformed into a transactional one. And that's exacerbated by a growing disenfranchised class, decaying inner cities, and a bankrupt educational system. Don't misunderstand me, Mr. Kantlowitz . . .

MERV: Kant, like the philosopher.

SARA: In many ways America is a brilliant country. But it's becoming as class-driven a society as this one.

MERV: So you're a hot-shot Jewish lady banker who's secretly a Marxist.

SARA: This is hardly the time to be a Marxist.

MERV: But your sister's right. You are a brilliant woman!

SARA: Excuse me, Mr. Kant, I really should check on my roast.

MERV: Are we having roast beef and Yorkshire pudding? Blimey, I've been hoping for a good old-fashioned, high-cholesterol English meal. I had a banger for breakfast this morning.

SARA *extends her hand:* It was lovely to meet you, Mr. Kant.

MERV: Whenever I come over here, I treat myself to one blow-out meal at Simpson's in the Strand.

SARA: Only Americans eat there. It's a tourist trap.

MERV: That's why I was so delighted when Geoffrey invited me here for dinner tonight.

SARA: Geoffrey did what?

MERV: And I said to myself, "Merv, this way you can avoid that tourist trap Simpson's in the Strand and have a good old-fashioned Anglo-Saxon Jewish meal."

SARA: How intimate are you with Geoffrey, Mr. Kant?

MERV: I'd say we have a close working relationship.

SARA: Oh?

MERV: When Geoffrey's musical *The Scarlet Pimpernel* came to New York last season, there arose during rehearsal an emergency need for signature chartreuse pelts. And while the British production blithely used dyed scarlet fox, the anti-fur lobby in New York pressed into early action. So my services were recommended by Geoffrey's producer, Mr. Bernard Lasker. And that was the beginning of a very beautiful friendship.

SARA: So you're a show biz furrier.

MERV: I was a show biz and novelty furrier. Now I am the world leader in synthetic animal protective covering. And Sara, to this day my one regret is that while the anti-furries were still picketing I didn't have Geoffrey sign over to me a quarter percent of that Pumpernickel. Next year I could be playing in Tokyo, Reykjavik, and forty-seven other cities worldwide.

SARA: Mr. Kant . . .

MERV: Please call me Merv. You call me Mr. Kant and I think I'm your high school principal. My hunch is we're roughly the same age.

SARA: Mr. Merv, today is my fifty-fourth birthday.

MERV: We are the same age. Roughly.

SARA: My sister Pfeni has flown here from Bombay, and my other sister, Gorgeous, is due in shortly from Newton, Massachusetts.

MERV: That's exactly why I want to come to your birthday party. Sounds like there'll be such interesting people here. I can't believe your father named you Sara and your other sister Gorgeous!

SARA: We're not just having a roast, actually. The roast is part of a cassoulet. That calls for beans, lamb, and duck and pork sausage. I don't recall the rules precisely, but if any of those go against your or the Rabbi of Dublin's religious or dietary regimen, you might want to get to Simpson's in the Strand after all.

MERV: And what will I tell Geoffrey?

SARA: That I behaved rather rudely and scared you away.

MERV: Do you tend to do that with men?

SARA: Are you a psychiatrist in addition to a furrier?

MERV: Shhh! Please, synthetic animal covering.

SARA: In answer to your question, yes, some men find me threatening.

MERV: My daughter tells me men find her threatening. Of course, when my daughter isn't in the Haifa parks, she's a captain in the Israeli army.

SARA: And your wife?

MERV: My wife was a Roslyn housewife. She died three years ago.

SARA: I'm sorry.

MERV: So was I. Her name was Helene and she wasn't very threatening, which is probably why my daughter is in the Israeli army. And you?

SARA: Me what?

MERV: Your husband.

SARA: My second is on his fifth wife. My first I've lost track of, and personally I doubt there will be a third.

MERV: So you've closed shop.

SARA: I'm a very busy woman, Mr. Merv. Would you excuse me? *Exits.*

MERV: Of course. Please make myself at home. *Looks at some books on a small table.* Sara, you've gotta lot of books about Disraeli here. Personally, I prefer Adlai Stevenson. Do you still have your Stevenson buttons, Sara? I keep mine with the ones from the Columbia Varsity Show of 1955. I played Madame Chiang Kai-shek. Actually, I think I would like a real drink, thanks. Scotch and water? Why not? *Pours himself a drink from the bar.* You know, I don't think it's particularly true that Jews don't drink. I think it's a myth made up by our mothers to persuade innocent women that Jewish men make superior husbands. In other words, it's worth it to put up with my crankiness, my hypochondria, my opinions on world problems, because I don't drink. *Takes a sip and begins looking through her records.* How about a little music, Sara? You have a lot of LPs. That's nice, I like a girl with LPs. CDs belong in the bank. Of course, I don't have to tell you that. I'm glad to see that you like Frank Sinatra and all the Broadway show tunes. I still cry at *Finian's Rainbow,* or is it *Brigadoon? Takes out two albums as* GORGEOUS, *a very pretty but overdone woman of around forty-six enters through the open door. She wears a fake Chanel suit with too many accessories, and carries imitation Louis Vuitton suitcases. He doesn't notice her.* Which one has "Look to the Rainbow"?

GORGEOUS: "Finian's Rainbow." You must be a friend of Geoffrey's.

MERV: How did you know?

GORGEOUS: All of Geoffrey's friends like musicals.

MERV: And you must be Gorgeous. We were just talking about you.

GORGEOUS: And how I got my name! Well, it's obvious, isn't it! Thanks for leaving the door open. I feel like Elijah.

MERV: I also just met your sister Pfeni.

GORGEOUS: Aren't my sisters fabulous? They're really such funsy people!

MERV: I wouldn't say your sister Sara is "funsy."

GORGEOUS: Maybe you should marry her.

MERV: I've only spent five minutes with her.

GORGEOUS: So what? Some people know at first sight. People call me from the Massachusetts Turnpike because they've just met someone at a rest stop and have fallen in love.

MERV: And you speak to these people?

GORGEOUS: Have you ever been to Boston?

MERV: My son lives there.

GORGEOUS: Well, if you ever listen to the radio when you visit your son, you'd know that everyone calls Dr. Gorgeous. *Begins to sing her theme song.*

> Call Dr. Gorgeous, ring, ring, ring,
> Call Dr. Gorgeous, ring, ring, ring.

Mimes picking up a phone.

"Hello, I'm Dr. Gorgeous, how can I help you?" Isn't that great! Isn't that funsy! I just have the best time. I'm sorry, I didn't catch your name.

MERV: Mervyn Kant.

"Thanks for leaving the door open. I feel like Elijah."
(Madeline Kahn) ©1992 Martha Swope

GORGEOUS *helps herself to nuts from a dish:* Merlin, let me tell you something. I was a Newton housewife with four wonderful kids. My husband, Henry, is a very prominent attorney. We have a very comfortable lifestyle. In other words, everything was going just great, but I needed just a little sparkle to make it all perfect.

MERV: So you're the sister who did everything right. You married the attorney, you had the children, you moved to the suburbs.

GORGEOUS: Now, don't make me into a cliché. I am much more than that. Merlin, I am one of the first real jugglers. I love nuts and they're just terrible for you. Ucch! I'm so fat! I ate like a pig! Honey, do me a favor, give me one more and then put these on the other table. Sara shouldn't keep things like this around the house. The Dr. Gorgeous Show is hoping to make the leap from radio to cable. You know that absolutely everything shows on television.

MERV: I'm sure you'll have no problem.

GORGEOUS: Sara, who is such a brilliant woman, says I could have a spectacular career in communications. Talking has always come easily to me.

MERV: Yes, you're very natural.

GORGEOUS: In fact, my first show really happened by accident. So many women in the Newton Temple Beth El sisterhood wanted to know how I managed in our frantic modern times to maintain a warm traditional home, that they begged me to give a speech to their local chapter. Well, as it happens, P. S., who should be in the audience but Rabbi Carl Pearlstein, the host of "Newton at Sunrise." Pearlstein was so impressed with my presentation that he invited me on his show.

MERV: I've heard of Pearlstein. Didn't he write *I Learned Everything but Handwriting in First Grade?*

GORGEOUS: Try *Learning to Love Again, Learning to Live Again*. Only twenty-six months on every bestseller list.

MERV: Of course. He was recently indicted.

GORGEOUS: Rabbi Pearlstein is a great man. His accountant was evil.

MERV: I think we use the same one. I'm sorry, please tell me what happened next.

GORGEOUS: I became a regular on Pearlstein's show. Then he was indicted, and the rest is history. Now you just mention Dr. Gorgeous anywhere in suburban Boston, Framingham, Natick, or Lynn, and they all know who I am. Merlin, I am what they call a real middle-aged success story. And I am having a ball. It's really funsy.

MERV: Your husband must be very proud.

GORGEOUS: He is thrilled. And so supportive.

MERV: I have only one more question. When did you become a doctor?

GORGEOUS: You've heard of Dr Pepper?

MERV: Yes.

GORGEOUS: So I'm Dr. Gorgeous. *Laughs and takes his arm.* Merlin, I loved talking to you. Geoffrey always has the most darling friends, although you're a little older than most of them. But I really must say hello to my sister. You know, my sister Sara is a brilliant woman. But she's also very vulnerable, very loving, very tender. She's had a hard year, she was ill, urgent female trouble, and couldn't come to our mother's funeral. That's why we're all here for her birthday. We're extremely close. *Calls.* Sara! *Turns back to* MERV. I adore my sisters. *Calls her again.* Sara! I'm here. Sara, it's me, Gorgeous.

SARA *enters.*

SARA, *very British:* Hallo Gorgeous!

GORGEOUS *imitates her:* Hallo Sara! *They embrace.* GOR-
GEOUS *looks over* SARA *in her apron.* Well, well, don't
you look glamorous!

SARA: Gorgeous, where's Henry?

GORGEOUS: He has a very heavy case load, and he wanted
to watch Lily play lacrosse. Merlin here was just telling
me what a handsome woman you are. I believe that men
really are looking for strong women these days. The decade of the bimbo is over. This is the nineties, Sara. This
is the era of the strong but feminine woman. Don't you
think so, Merlin?

MERV: I think I should go back to the Savoy to freshen up.

GORGEOUS: Why don't you freshen up downstairs? That's
where Geoffrey always goes. *Winks at him.* But I'm sure
you knew that.

SARA: I don't think he did, actually. He's Geoffrey's New
York furrier.

GORGEOUS: How fabulous! Are they picketing outside?

MERV: I'm afraid, Gorgeous, that you've made me out to be
a far more interesting man than I really am.

GORGEOUS: I'm sure you're a very interesting man. Some of
the most interesting men I know in Newton, Massachusetts are furriers.

SARA: How many furriers do you know in Newton, Massachusetts exactly?

GORGEOUS: I'm sure there are more than a few.

SARA: Yes, but how many do you actually know?

GORGEOUS: Well, there's mine, Monsieur Joseph of Newton,
and Lily's friend Jonah Mazzarelli's father was a furrier

at Jordan Marsh. And Henry once did a furrier's bankruptcy.

MERV: Oh, Jesus.

SARA: And all of them, Messieurs Joseph and Mazzarelli and Henry's bankruptcy, are among the most interesting men in Newton!

GORGEOUS: Sara, I'm tired!

SARA: I am asking you to be specific. I am asking you to take responsibility for whatever it is you babble about. Life is serious business, Gorgeous. Life isn't funsy.

GORGEOUS *takes out a gift from a shopping bag:* Happy birthday, Sara. I'll stay with my ladies. *Picks up her suitcase and her purse.*

SARA: Oh, here we go again. At least say hello to Pfeni.

GORGEOUS: Is Pfeni still sleeping with Geoffrey?

SARA: Yes.

GORGEOUS: Then I don't need to see Pfeni.

SARA: Gorgeous!

GORGEOUS: Don't you think it's time she considered someone even remotely available? Don't you think it's time she stopped living her life like she was on an extended junior year abroad?

MERV: Maybe you could help her. You help so many people.

GORGEOUS: That's true. I do. Thank you, Mervyn.

MERV: Thank you for not calling me the magician.

GORGEOUS: I'll stay for dinner if you will.

MERV: Sara?

SARA: I can put the sausage on a different plate.

MERV: Ladies, would you please excuse me. I'm going downstairs to change my shirt.

GORGEOUS: Why don't you use the guest room upstairs? It's much cozier.

MERV: Thank you. Who knows? Tonight could be funsy.
Exits upstairs.

GORGEOUS: I like him.

SARA: He's a certain type.

GORGEOUS: You've become a hard woman, Sara.

SARA: I can't be surprised about things I already know.

GORGEOUS: Rabbi Pearlstein says he has great hope for you.
He says you need a man to make you soft again.

SARA: You know what Tessie says when she can't bear to
listen to me for a moment longer? "Mommy, I am going
to throw up!" Gorgeous, I am going to throw up!

GORGEOUS: Rabbi Pearlstein is a very wise man.

SARA: Then tell him to concentrate on his income tax. Besides, there is someone in my life. Nick Pym's coming
for dinner tonight.

GORGEOUS: Nick Pym is a Nazi.

SARA: Nick Pym can trace his lineage back to the Duke of
Marlborough.

GORGEOUS: That's fine, sweetsie, but we can't. He's a phi-
landerer and a Nazi.

SARA: He was a Thatcher M. P. and he dates a few other
women.

GORGEOUS: You said he screws a lot of other women.

SARA: I never said that!

GORGEOUS: Well, I didn't hear it at the Safeway in Newton!
Who knows, he could be just the ticket. Sara, the experts tell me that after your kind of "procedure" it's very
important for you to get back on the saddle.

SARA: In the saddle.

GORGEOUS: You're not the only woman who's been ill. I
read in *Newsweek*, it's now at least three in ten.

SARA: Really! That's quite a sisterhood. Even bigger than
Hadassah.

GORGEOUS: Female Trouble is going to be the health issue of the decade.

SARA: Female Trouble? There are real words, Gorgeous. Ovarian abscess. Hysterectomy. According to all experts, I am now happily recovered and shall survive.

GORGEOUS: Do you want to share your anger, your rage?

SARA: Actually, I prefer to get on with my life.

GORGEOUS: Rabbi Pearlstein says we should openly discuss our feelings.

SARA: I can't tell you what a comfort it is to live in a country where "our feelings" are openly repressed. End of conversation, Gorgeous!

GORGEOUS: Fine. Have it your way. Achhhh! My feet are killing me. *Slips her shoes off and lies on the couch.* I schlepped twenty ladies through Harrods and up and down Sloane Street. One of them, Mrs. Hershkovitz, her daughter was a counselor at Lily's summer camp, everywhere she goes she has to have another piece of Wedgwood. She's got Wedgwood clocks, Wedgwood bells, Wedgwood napkin holders, and meanwhile her daughter was the biggest dope dealer at Camp Pinehurst.

SARA, *laughing:* I don't know how you do it. I couldn't put up with them.

GORGEOUS: Believe me, Sara, they wouldn't like you either.

SARA: Oh, God, I'm sure not.

GORGEOUS *picks up shoe:* I don't mind, really. The one thing that bothers me is my feet. I told Henry if I get this cable job, the first thing I'm going to do is stop wearing cheap shoes. I'm marching myself right into Saks and treating myself to Bruno Maglis, Ferragamos, and Manulo Blanchikis.

SARA: Manulo who?

GORGEOUS: Manulo Blahnik. Whatever. It's all the brands

the ladies in my group tell me are the best. Do you know, those bitches—achh, I shouldn't use that kind of language—what those ladies said to me this morning. "Gorgeous, you're a celebrity now. Why don't you treat yourself to a real Chanel suit? You're such a brilliant and attractive woman, it kills us to see you with an imitation Louis Vuitton purse." Do you know how much one of those Chanel suits costs? Sara, you're my brilliant big sister, when we were growing up, why didn't Daddy tell us about money?

SARA: Because girls weren't supposed to know about money.

GORGEOUS: But you became a banker.

SARA: That's because no one ever called me Gorgeous. *Kisses* GORGEOUS' *forehead and begins to stroke her hair.*

GORGEOUS: I'm so tired, Sara. So very tired. Up a little higher. Mmmm. That feels so good. Remember when Mother stroked our hair?

SARA: I remember coming home with a 99 and her shrieking at me, "Where's the other point?"

GORGEOUS: Mother really missed saying good-bye to you.

SARA: Mother and I had a Female Trouble conflict.

GORGEOUS: She wanted to see us all happy.

SARA: We are happy, Gorgeous. It's just not our mother's kind of happiness. I wonder why Tessie isn't back yet.

GORGEOUS: What time is it?

SARA: Around 7:45.

GORGEOUS: But the sun's just going down.

SARA: " 'Tis dark and dreary, this sepulchral isle. This royal throne of kings."

GORGEOUS *stands up and puts on her shoes:* Oh my God! We have to light the candles.

SARA: Why? We have electricity.

GORGEOUS: Sara. It's the Sabbath sundown. Where are your candles?

SARA: I have two Asprey candelabras in the dining room.

GORGEOUS: What about those two on the mantelpiece?

SARA: Majolica. Victorian, I believe, 1893.

GORGEOUS: I need a tichkel for my head.

SARA: I doubt I have that.

GORGEOUS: All right. Just a napkin.

SARA: Cloth or paper?

GORGEOUS: Sara, the sun's going down.

SARA: Here, take this. *Gives her a cloth from India that* PFENI *left on the couch.*

GORGEOUS: Matches?

SARA: Can't we wait for my birthday cake?

GORGEOUS: Sara, remember the Sabbath Day and keep it holy. *Lights the candles.*

SARA: I can't tell you how many Sabbath sundowns have come and gone here without lighting candles. And guess what? The next morning the sun comes right back up again.

GORGEOUS *prays over the candles:* Baruch ahtah adonai! elohenu! melech ha-olam!

TESS *and* TOM, *twenty, a working-class hero with spiked hair and black boots, enter. He cuts off* GORGEOUS's *prayer.*

TOM: Hello, Mrs. Goode, are you having a seance?

SARA: Hello, Tom. Tessie.

TOM: I love Stonehenge.

GORGEOUS: Shh! *Continues to pray.* Asher! kiddish! shanu b'mitzvosov!

TOM: Why is she wearing a dishtowel on her head?

TESS: Shh.

SARA: Tessie's aunt is performing an ancient tribal ritual.

GORGEOUS *looks at Sara:* Vit zi vahnu! lehadlik nehr!

PFENI *enters:* Tessie, I just went to meet you. Sorry, Gorgeous!

SARA: I told you you'd be late.

GORGEOUS: Sara, I am not finished!

SARA: Tessie, shh! Your aunt isn't finished.

GORGEOUS *completes the prayer:* Shel Shabbas. Amen.

SARA: Finished now?

GORGEOUS: You've become a hard woman, Sara! *Picks up her suitcase and charges upstairs.*

TESS: Mother, how could you do that?

SARA: Do what? What is this to you? If we had a Muslim visiting here, you wouldn't suddenly bow down to Mecca.

TESS: But this is important to Aunt Gorgeous.

SARA: Pfeni, blow out the candles.

PFENI: But Gorgeous just lit them.

SARA: Stop being the good little sister and blow out the goddamned candles! PFENI *blows out the candles. It is suddenly dark in the room.* TESS *runs upstairs.* Drinks here in the sitting room at half-past.

SCENE 3

Around 8:30 P.M. Frank Sinatra is playing on the stereo.
NICHOLAS PYM, *an extremely well groomed British gentleman of about fifty-eight, enters from the dining room.* TOM *comes down the stairs. They eye each other as* PYM *turns off the Sinatra.* TESS *enters from the kitchen in blue jeans.*

TESS: It's just like my mother to have a dinner party on the night the Soviet Union is falling apart.

TOM: A crowd in Vilnius tore down the statue of Lenin today. It's amazing.

TESS: Mr. Pym, are you aware that fifty years of Soviet occupation has inflicted environmental damage that will cost the people of Lithuania at least one hundred and fifty billion dollars to repair?

NICK PYM: Tell me something, Tessie, where does this passion for the Baltics come from?

TOM: My dad is from Lithuania. And me uncles and me aunties still live there.

NICK PYM: There's a decent old restaurant in Vilnius.

TESS: The Old Cellar. My Aunt Pfeni already told me.

NICK PYM: Tessie, my luv, do you think the state of Kentucky is viable without the United States?

TOM: Lithuania has a culture and people independent from the Soviets.

NICK PYM: So does Kentucky. Think about the Derby.

TESS: If Western culture is to survive at all, Mr. Pym, one has to look beyond the States, England, France, or Germany. As it is, I feel completely irrelevant coming of age as a white European female.

NICK PYM: Tess, dear, I'm terribly sorry.

TESS: It could be worse. I could be a white European male.

Enter SARA *with a tray. She wears elegant hostess clothes.*

SARA: As promised, a few little nibblies.

TESS: Nibblies?

SARA: Hors d'oeuvries. Nick?

NICK PYM: They look marvelous, darling. Tom and Tessie were just sharing with me their excitement over the demise of the Soviet Union.

TESS: Well, mother, everything in Eastern Europe is going to change.

NICK PYM: I'd say it depends on the particular countries, actually. For instance, the Hungarians have always been industrious. This is marvelous cheese, darling!

SARA: New kind of chevre from the place on Wilton Street.

TOM: What's chevre?

SARA: Form of goat, dear. Would you care for some?

TOM: No thanks, Mrs. Goode. I don't much like cheese unless it's yellow. I only eat primary color foods, ma'am.

SARA: When Tessie was in nursery school, her favorite food was sushi. But Tessie's always had a sophisticated palette.

TESS: That's not true, mother. I only eat fish and chips and hamburgers.

MERV *enters singing:* Zip-pa-dee-do-dah, I love my new shirt! Good evening everyone. I'm Merv Kant.

NICK PYM *stands up:* Nick Pym. How do you do.

MERV: And you must be Tessie, and Tom the Lithuanian nationalist. You know, before the Holocaust, Vilnius was home to about 65,000 Jews.

SARA: Can I get you a drink, Merv?

MERV: Tessie, I suspect your mother is one of those hostesses who prefers that a guest not come into a room and immediately bring the conversation around to the Holocaust. I'll have a scotch, please.

NICK PYM: At least it's not English politics, the EEC, or the personal lives of the bloody royals.

MERV: That's true. It could be worse, Sara. I could chat about leopardette—that's my fall leopard line.

TOM: Fantastic.

NICK PYM: Oh, are you a furrier?

SARA: In addition to being Geoffrey's very talented New York furrier, Mr. Kant has recently been visiting Eastern Europe with the American Jewish Confederacy.

MERV: Congress.

NICK PYM: Were they all furriers, too?

MERV *pauses to look at* PYM: No.

NICK PYM: Please tell us, Merv, what did you find on your travels?

MERV: Tessie, do you remember an event in modern history called the Concert of Europe?

TESS: Count Metternich's plan to reestablish stability in Europe after Napoleon. 1815.

TOM: Tessie's really smart, Mrs. Goode. She's the brains in our family. *Nestles* TESS. SARA *turns away.*

MERV *smiles at* SARA: Like mother, like daughter.

TESS: Metternich's goal was nationalism.

SARA, *very quickly:* And, specifically, creating an alliance between England, Austria, Russia, and Prussia.

NICK PYM: Another disastrous European economic community!

SARA: Completely different circumstances, Nick.

MERV: Bankers have to wait. The historians haven't finished. And Tessie, what always goes hand in hand with European nationalism?

TOM: American movies and CNN?

MERV: Sorry, Tom, the answer is anti-Semitism.

NICK PYM: That's a sweeping generalization.

MERV: You asked me what I found on my travels. What I found was sweeping, but unfortunately true. Pick a country—any country, Russia, France, Austria, Hungary—it remains from before Count Metternich to I'm sure centuries from now a soft but never silent refrain. And that, Tessie, is the true concert of Europe. In Britain, of course, it's all handled a little more politely.

NICK PYM: That's bloody nonsense. Jews have been at the financial core of England for generations.

SARA: I always liked Metternich. If I wasn't promised to Disraeli, I think we would have made a rather nice couple.

MERV: But, Sara, do I have a point about England? You're a Jewish woman living in London.

SARA: I really don't have an opinion about this.

TESS: Why not?

SARA: Because this isn't about us, honey.

TOM: I thought Tessie was Jewish.

SARA: She is. But Mr. Kant is really talking about families in Russia and Eastern Europe who are unable to practice their religion.

TOM: I hate the Soviets.

SARA: That aside, if Tessie chooses to practice her religion in England, she perfectly well can.

NICK PYM: For that matter, she could go to the East End for a gefilte sandwich.

SARA: You'd like them, Tom. They're a fish cake, very much like quenelles.

TESS: Mother, would you stop it!

SARA: What am I doing?

TESS: Mother, if you don't leave Tom alone, we're leaving.

GORGEOUS *sweeps into the room. She is in fake Ungaro cocktail wear, with accessories.*

GORGEOUS: Good evening! Good evening!

NICK PYM *rises:* Gorgeous, you look absolutely smashing!

TOM: Maybe she should change her name to Smashing!

GORGEOUS: Well, well, well, this looks like a funsy little group.

NICK PYM: We've been having the most marvelous time chatting about anti-Semitism and the Concert of Europe.

GORGEOUS: Which concert is that? I must have missed it.

SARA: It's all right, Gorgeous. It took place in 1815.

GORGEOUS: You know, I'm taking a music appreciation class now at the Boston Symphony. Why are all those opera singers so overweight? Honestly, I don't know how they breathe, much less sing. Is that goat cheese? Blech. I hate goat cheese. *Kisses* TESS. Tessie, Tessie, you look so beautiful. Isn't my niece beautiful? I'm sorry, I forgot your name.

TOM: Tom.

GORGEOUS: Isn't my niece beautiful, Tom? My daughters are all desperately jealous of Tessie. Of all the cousins she was always the prettiest and the brightest. But I tell them to just make the most of what they've got. I knew girls who were just like Tessie in high school—beautiful, talented, bright—who have had such difficult times in later life. Tessie, carpe diem; now's the time to enjoy.

SARA: Gorgeous, would you like a drink?

GORGEOUS: Did I say something wrong? I'm always saying something wrong.

The lights flash up and down. GEOFFREY *appears on the steps in evening clothes and a plumed hat. He puts on rhinestone glasses.*

GEOFFREY: Ladies and gentlemen! In honor of our kindest innkeeper Sara Goode's birthday, and the collapse this very day of the Soviet Union, my beloved Pfeni Rosensweig and I have prepared an evening's entertainment with a very special guest. Ladies and gentlemen, it is my honor to present to you, after almost a century of hiding in a Santa Monica post office, her royal highness the Grand Duchess Anastasia Rosensweig Romanov.

PFENI *comes down the steps in a ball gown and tiara:* Das Vi Danya.

SARA: Pfeni, that's my good evening gown!

PFENI: Da! I am here to celebrate the name day of my sister Sara Goode Romanov.

GEOFFREY: Don't forget about your other sister, the eminent Petrograd physician, Dr. Gorgeous "Noodles" Romanov.

GORGEOUS: They're always making fun of me, Merv.

GEOFFREY: But stay, gentle "Noodles," who is this Murf that you so spritely call on? And see his amazing technicolor shirt of many colors.

NICK PYM: Bravo, Geoffrey! So many Jewish American men I know, professionals mostly, wear those shirts. Why is that, Merv?

MERV: It's a money-lending uniform.

NICK PYM: Beg your pardon.

MERV: They're so well designed, you'd never know it costs a pound of flesh to get them.

SARA *looks at* PYM *as the room laughs with* MERV: Geoffrey, what's happened to our play?

GORGEOUS, *applauding:* We want our play! We want our play!

NICK PYM: Bring on the elves and the faerie sprites!

MERV: Bring on the beautiful dancing girls!

SARA: Bring on the Scarlet Pimpernel!

All shout "Pimpernel! The Pimpernel!"

GEOFFREY *sings:*

> They seek him here,
> They seek him there,
> Those Frenchies seek him everywhere.

ALL *sing:* I knew him well, I knew him well, the Scarlet Pimpernel!

GEOFFREY *gets* TOM *up and puts the plumed hat on him.*

TOM: I love being in your house, Tessie!

GEOFFREY *kneels in front of* SARA: Milady, I have been dispatched twelve days on horseback by your sisters to wish you the happiest, merriest, jolliest birthday ever . . . hip, hip . . .

"I knew him well, I knew him well, the Scarlet Pimpernel!"
(Julie Dretzin, Robert Klein, Patrick Fitzgerald, John Vickery, Jane
Alexander, Frances McDormand, Madeline Kahn) © 1992 Martha Swope

ALL: Hooray!

GEOFFREY: Hip, hip . . .

ALL: Hooray! Speech . . . speech!

SARA: Thank you. Thank you. I feel truly fortunate tonight to have my beautiful daughter and my family and friends with me. And Geoffrey, my baby sister is right. You do add texture to my life.

GEOFFREY: Long live Sara Goode.

ALL: Long live Sara Goode.

SARA: Long live the Scarlet Pimpernel.

GEOFFREY: And all his touring companies!

ALL: And all his touring companies!

SARA: Dinner is served.

GEOFFREY: "Once more unto the breach, dear friends."

TOM, TESS, GORGEOUS, PFENI, *and* NICK PYM *march behind* GEOFFREY. *They sing:*

> They seek him here,
> They seek him there,
> Those Frenchies seek him everywhere.

GORGEOUS *sings:*

> I knew him well!
> I knew him well!

They march into the dining room. MERV *stays behind and watches* SARA *as she clears the hors d'oeuvres. He joins in as all the others continue to sing.*

> Ding the bells go dong,
> Hear the maiden's song,
> I knew him well.

MERV: You're not singing.
SARA: I only do show tunes from the fifties.

TOM, TESS, GORGEOUS, PFENI, NICK PYM, GEOFFREY *in the dining room, singing,* MERV *singing directly to* SARA:

The Scarlet Pimpernel!

MERV: Sara, you really know how to throw a good Shabbes!

SARA *looks up from her tray. The lights fade as she joins the others in the dining room. They sit down to a gracious dinner.*

SCENE 4

After dinner: around 11:30. GEOFFREY, PFENI, SARA, MERVYN, NICK PYM, TESS, *and* TOM *enter, laughing hysterically, from the dining room.* GORGEOUS *clears the dishes.*

GEOFFREY, *still laughing:* Yes, yes. It's true.

SARA: No.

GEOFFREY, *laughing:* Wait, there's more. So, Danny Kaye. So Danny Kaye dresses up as a customs inspector. And! And Sir Larry! I'm sorry!

TOM: Who's Sir Larry?

SARA: Laurence Olivier, Tom. He was in the movie, *Marathon Man.*

TESS: Mother!

GEOFFREY: So Danny Kaye supposedly dresses up like a customs inspector at the New York airport, and when Sir Larry comes through, he calls him aside into a special room, strips him buck naked, and inspects every single bloody part of him!

SARA: Why? Was he smuggling?

GEOFFREY: Sara, they were, as we say, "very close personal friends."

SARA: Danny Kaye! As in Hans Christian Andersen!

GEOFFREY: And then apparently they went off and spent a very warm and funsy night at the Saint Regis.

SARA: Has this been documented?

GEOFFREY: Who gives a damn?

GORGEOUS, *coming into the room from the dining area carrying four glasses:* Sara, does your crystal go in the dishwasher?

SARA: Gorgeous, please stop. You don't have to do that.

GEOFFREY *looks at his watch:* Well, I'm afraid we must be going.

PFENI: We must?

GEOFFREY: Hollywood people are in town, my darling, and I'm afraid I agreed to meet for late drinks at The Groucho with the producers of *Body Heat.*

TOM: *Body Heat?* You mean Kathleen Turner?

GEOFFREY: Well, it's the stage version. Tommy, I'm the only theatre director who can ignite the stage with true female sexuality.

SARA: Since when are you the expert on female sexuality?

GEOFFREY: Did you see my Cleopatra? Or my Lulu? Love is love, Sara. Gender is merely spare parts. Just ask Danny Kaye.

PFENI *and* GEOFFREY *exit.*

TOM: Isn't it late for a meeting?

MERV: Geoffrey's always working, Tom. He and I once walked right past a shootout on Broadway. The police yelled "Take cover," and Geoffrey asked me if I thought he should do *Showboat* for television.

SARA: That's a musical, Tom.

TESS: Mother.

GORGEOUS, *carrying napkin holders in a gold basket:* It was a great musical, Tom. Here, Sara, I didn't know where to put this. Everything's put away now. *Puts the basket on the mantelpiece.* You don't have to thank me. It's been such a funsy evening, but I'm exhausted. G'mbye, you lovely people.

ALL: Goodnight.

TOM: Goodnight, Aunt Gorgeous.

GORGEOUS: Goodnight, dear. *Exits up the stairs.*

NICK PYM: I think I'd better be leaving as well.

SARA: You can't stay for another port?

NICK PYM: Darling, you're too kind. But I'm meeting my niece early in the morning.

TESS: Your niece?

MERV: We all love our nieces, Tessie.

NICK PYM: Fabulous, darling. *Gives her a gift.* Happy birthday. Merv. Good-bye, Tom. Good-bye, Tessie. Good luck in Latvia, darling. You know the shocking thing about all this business with the Soviets is one questions what in God's name the entire twentieth century was for. Good night. *Exits.*

TESS: People like him are what's wrong with this country.

SARA: Tessie, that's a ridiculous statement.

TESS: But it's true. The man has no commitments.

SARA: The man doesn't have your commitments.

TESS: Mother, he's dating the best friend of a girl in my class. He's one of those weirdo English bankers who takes sixteen-year-old models to dinner at Annabel's and then goes home alone and puts panty hose over his head and dances to *Parsifal*.

SARA: Tessie, you have no business saying things like that.

TOM: What's *Parsifal?*

SARA: It's a Wagner opera, Tom.

TESS: Come on, Tom.

SARA: Where are you going?

TESS: Upstairs.

TOM: There's a candlelight vigil tomorrow in Hyde Park. We're coordinating.

SARA: And you have to do that now?

TESS: Mother, would you like a rundown of our schedule?

SARA: No, I wouldn't. Good night, dear. Good night, Tom.

TOM: Great party, Mrs. Goode. That stew was brilliant.

SARA: It was a cassoulet, dear. Good night.

They exit upstairs.

MERV: The duck was very bright too. I'd say at least 150 I.Q.

SARA *begins straightening the living room.*

SARA: Aren't you going home to bed too? It's very late.

MERV: Not when I can watch you clean.

SARA: You enjoy watching women clean?

MERV: I enjoy watching women who don't need to clean, clean.

SARA: Actually, I have to clean. The help is on vacation and I like a tidy household.

MERV: Just like your mother.

SARA: My mother never cleaned. When I came home from college, she made an effort and pushed all the laundry under the bed.

MERV: But I bet she was a great cook.

SARA: She never cooked. We all went out to dinner every night at Sparky's family restaurant.

MERV: Was your mother Jewish?

SARA: For a supposedly intelligent man you have a persistently narrow perspective.

MERV: Thank you.

SARA: Excuse me.

MERV: You called me intelligent; I didn't know that you noticed.

SARA: I know you, Merv. You're just like all the other men I went to high school with. You're smart, you're a good provider, you read *The Times* every day, you started running at fifty to recapture your youth, you worry a little too much about your health, you thought about having affairs, but you never actually did it, and now that she's departed, your late wife Roslyn is a saint.

MERV: Her name was Helene. We lived in Roslyn.

SARA: And I'm sure you traveled and I'm sure your children are very nice people, and Merv, if my sisters or I had any sense, we would all have married you too.

MERV: What about Gorgeous? I thought she did marry me. Old Henry sounds like a nice enough guy: lawyer, good father, stays home to watch the kids play lacrosse.

SARA *begins dusting the mantelpiece:* Yes, Henry's wonderful, and I'm sure you're wonderful, and Tom's wonderful. You're all wonderful. *Knocks over the napkin rings.* God damn it, Gorgeous!

MERV: Hey, hey, take it easy. Take it easy.

SARA: You know what really irritates me in life, Merv? When men like you tell women to take it easy because somewhere they believe that all women are innately hysterics.

MERV: Why won't you give me a break?

SARA: Why won't you please just go home! *She starts to cry suddenly. He puts his arm around her.*

MERV: It's all right. I promise.

SARA *laughs slightly and moves away:* Now you're really

convinced all women are hysterics. I'm sorry. Really. Tessie says I should take stress tabs.

MERV: You're fine. Let's talk about something else. How 'bout the American class system. Or, I've got a lively topic: Count Metternich and the Concert of Europe. Sadie, my lips haven't formed those words since I was a senior in high school.

SARA: Why did you call me Sadie?

MERV: You called me Mr. Kantlowitz. And Gorgeous called me Merlin the Magician. I figure anything goes in this house.

SARA: My grandfather called me Sadie. Sara was too biblical for him. He hoped I'd grow up to be a singer.

MERV: So you do sing!

SARA: When I was at Radcliffe. I was with a girls' singing group. The Cliffe Clef. I was a Cleffie!

MERV: Can I hear a little?

SARA: Merv, we're too old for this.

MERV: For what?

SARA: You're a very nice man. But you're not my type.

MERV: Sadie, you're not mine either. You're not what I'd call a warm or accessible woman.

SARA: Unlike the wonderful Roslyn.

MERV: Unlike the wonderful Roslyn. Tell me something, when did you figure out that you had all the answers?

SARA: High school. I knew what the teacher was going to ask before she asked it. I knew what was going to become of every girl in my class, and I knew, for some reason, I was different from them.

MERV: You weren't a nice Jewish girl.

SARA: Why do you always come back to that?

MERV: I have a limited repertoire. I'm not as smart as you are, Sadie. I didn't get double 800's on my College Boards.

SARA: When we took those tests, they didn't publish the results.

MERV: But I'm sure the school called your mother just to let her know. What? So I'm right.

SARA: It was no big deal.

MERV: Of course it was a big deal. I'll bet the valedictorian was nowhere as intelligent as you.

SARA: Sonia Kirschenblatt. Went to Bryn Mawr, married an astronomy professor, lives in Princeton, works for educational testing.

MERV: Fuzzy brown hair. Poodle skirts. Started going to Greenwich Village bookstores at sixteen.

SARA: You knew her?

MERV: Her parents had a cabana at the Brighton Beach Baths. I was a cabana boy. I shtupped her the year before she went to Bryn Mawr.

SARA: So Sonia Kirschenblatt went to Bryn Mawr not a virgin.

MERV: It was no big deal.

SARA: Are you kidding? Thirty years ago it was a very big deal.

MERV: Look, thank God she didn't get pregnant or today I'd be an astronomy professor at Princeton. I like talking to you, Sadie. I wish you'd stop pushing the ashtray back and forth and maybe your shoulders could come down from your ears. *Starts to rub her shoulders.* I didn't think they could get any higher. Pretty soon they'll be on the ceiling.

SARA: Merv, do you want to "shtup" me tonight in Queen Anne's Gate, like you did Sonia Kirschenblatt that hot and lusty summer night at the Brighton Beach Baths?

MERV: We did it at Columbia in my dorm room in John Jay Hall.

"I like talking to you, Sadie."
(Robert Klein, Jane Alexander)

© 1992 Martha Swope

SARA: They didn't allow women in Columbia rooms then.

MERV: Sonia was a woman of great ingenuity. She didn't get to be valedictorian by being a half-wit.

SARA: But she wasn't so smart, either. She just worked hard. *Gets up from the couch.* Look, Merv, if you're thinking, "I know who this woman is sitting next to me. I grew up with her, with women like her, only sometime in her life she decided to run away. She moved to England, she dyed her hair, she named her daughter Tess and sent her to Westminster. She assimilated beyond her wildest dreams, and now she's lonely and wants to come home," you're being too obvious. Yes, I'm lonely, but I don't want to come home.

MERV: What about connect, Sadie?

SARA: Connect?

MERV: Connect, to another person.

SARA: How many support groups did you join when Roslyn died? I'm sorry, that was cruel.

MERV: No, but it was in surprisingly bad taste. I joined two, plus last year I went on Outward Bound to find myself on a cliff on Prince Edward Island.

SARA: And what did you learn about yourself?

MERV: That I couldn't write poetry. That I couldn't solve the Middle East with a Merv Kant peace plan. That I wasn't a particularly original thinker. And that more than anything I wanted to be in love again.

SARA: To have someone take care of you.

MERV: Listen, my wife wasn't named Roslyn and she wasn't a saint. She drank a little, she was depressed, a little, and she thought she could have been a contender if it wasn't for me. She put me through school, she brought up the children, and finally she got to take art classes at the museum four years before she died. Is that fair to a talented, intelligent woman? Sadie, I've already done having someone take care of me.

SARA: I'm sorry. I guess I'm the one who's being too obvious.

MERV: Thank you.

SARA: You're welcome.

MERV: I still believe there can be happiness in life, Sara. Brief but a moment or two.

SARA: Who's to say what's happy?

MERV: Are you?

SARA: It's not so bad. I'm looking forward to Tessie going to college and selling the house for a cozy flat.

MERV: And sex?

SARA: I miss sex. I always liked sex.

MERV: What about Lord Gefilte?

SARA: You heard Tessie. His taste runs to younger women.

MERV: I think you're gorgeous.

SARA: My sister is Gorgeous.

MERV: No, you are, Sara Rosensweig.

SARA *laughs:* Jesus. No one's called me that in thirty years. *He kisses her somewhat passionately.* I could never love you, Merv. And I'm old enough now and kind enough not to let you love me. But Merv, just for one night I could be Sonia Kirschenblatt at the Brighton Beach Baths and you a Columbia sophomore.

MERV: You think I have the energy of a Columbia sophomore?

SARA: I certainly hope so, Merv.

She starts to lead him up the stairs. He stops suddenly.

MERV: Sadie, I do have one request.

SARA: What?

MERV: Would you sing for me?

SARA: Merv, I . . .

MERV: I'll sing with you. I'm a wonderful singer. I was Mrs. Chiang Kai-shek in the Columbia Varsity Show of 1955.

SARA: So I heard.

MERV: You don't have to do anything fancy. I would just like it very much if I could hear you sing.

SARA: Merv, I have every Sinatra song ever recorded. How 'bout we let Frank sing?

MERV: But he was never a Cliffe Clef.

SARA: Please, Merv, pick a Sinatra song and let's go upstairs.

MERV *puts on "Just the Way You Look Tonight." He begins singing:*

> Lovely, don't you ever change,
> Keep that breathless charm . . ."
> Take it, Sara . . .

SARA, *quietly:* Merv, I just can't sing for you.

MERV *touches her face and begins leading her upstairs, singing:*

> Just the way you look tonight.

ACT TWO

S CENE *1*

Early Saturday morning. GEOFFREY, *in a Save the Rose T-shirt and turquoise underwear, is dancing and lipsynching to The Four Tops, singing "Sugar Pie Honey Bunch." He does some choreographed spots and turns.*

GEOFFREY:

> Sugar Pie Honey Bunch,
> You know that I love you,
> Can't help myself,
> I love you and nobody else.
> In and out of my life,
> You come and you go,
> Leaving only your picture behind,
> And I've kissed it a thousand times!

PFENI *comes up from her apartment and stares at him. He notices her.* Ladies and gentlemen, my favorite dancing partner, the lovely and talented "Pfeni"!

They dance together. They are both wonderful dancers. Suddenly PFENI *falls onto the sofa.*

PFENI: Geoffrey, it's six o'clock in the morning.

GEOFFREY: My darling, they'll never pick us for the ice follies if you don't practice. How can anyone be disparaging about American culture when you produced The Temptations, The Miracles, and The Four Tops? Every Holland/Dosier/Holland Motown song is brilliant, simply brilliant. "Sugar Pie Honey Bunch, you know that I love you" is comparable in every way to "Shall I compare thee to a summer's day."

PFENI: Geoffrey . . .

GEOFFREY: In fact, I'd much prefer to be a sugar pie honey bunch than a summer's day. Less elitist.

PFENI: Geoffrey . . . It's 6:12 in the morning.

GEOFFREY: That's the wonderful thing about this music, my angel. It's perfect for any and all social occasions! O.K., Miss U.S.A., for two hundred points, can you name the Four Tops? Time's up. Take it, U.K. Yes, Lady Bracknell. "The Four Tops are Levi Stubbs, Abdul 'Duke' Fakir, Lawrence Payton, and Renaldo 'Obie' Benson. They were all born and raised in Detroit, the Motor City, and the first time they entertained was at a high school graduation party in 1954." Congratulations, Lady Bracknell. You just won a two-week vacation for two to downtown Detroit and a year's supply of McVittie's digestive biscuits. *Pulls* PFENI *back up.*

PFENI: Geoffrey!

GEOFFREY: Ding! Ding! Ding! Ladies and gentlemen, the interval is now over. Please take your seats. This morning's performance will resume in one minute. *Turns the record back up even louder and begins dancing.*

Baby, I need your loving.
Got to have all your loving . . .

PFENI *turns the music off.*

PFENI: Geoffrey.

GEOFFREY: Come in, Big Ben.

PFENI: Geoffrey, it's now 6:16 in the morning and you're dancing around my big sister's house in your underwear.

GEOFFREY: I didn't want to wake you up.

PFENI: What about Sara?

GEOFFREY: I believe she's otherwise engaged.

PFENI: She is?

GEOFFREY: Your sister is a desirable woman. *Grabs* PFENI. She's related to you.

PFENI: You mean Sara and Merv. That's impossible.

GEOFFREY: Nothing is impossible, my darling. Look at us.

PFENI: I just thought he wasn't her . . .

GEOFFREY: Well, no one thinks you're my . . .

PFENI: Stop it, Geoffrey.

GEOFFREY *embraces her:* Pfeni, I'm a closet heterosexual.

PFENI: Well, I certainly haven't told anyone except my sisters.

GEOFFREY: And what do they think?

PFENI: They both wish they had met you first.

GEOFFREY *kisses* PFENI *on the forehead:* You're a wonderful person, Pfeni Rosensweig. I will never forget you. *Begins walking around the room.* Where is that damned Susie Cooper?

PFENI: Who?

GEOFFREY: I'm taking Jordan to the country this afternoon, and I have to find that plate of his that I loaned to your sister for Boxing Day. He's always nudging me for it.

"Pfeni, I'm a closet heterosexual."
(Francis McDormand, John Vickery)

© 1992 Martha Swope

How was I to know it was a limited edition Susie Cooper?

PFENI: Is Jordan still with Rum-Tum-Tugger?

GEOFFREY: Who?

PFENI: The cat.

GEOFFREY: Oh, Ian. Yes, he says he's quite happy with him.

PFENI: That's nice. Is Ian joining you in the country also?

GEOFFREY: Stop it, Pfeni.

PFENI: Stop what?

GEOFFREY: Jordan is my best friend. Stop making our lives more complicated than they already are.

PFENI: Your life isn't complicated. You do exactly what you want.

GEOFFREY: And you don't? My luv, you're the one who's always popping in from Bombay. You're the one who had me up all last night watching the reruns of Kurds hurling themselves into their children's early graves. There I am in bed with the woman I love, knowing she'd rather be in Kurdland. *Starts to sing,*

Come on along and listen to,
the lullaby of Kurdland!

PFENI *cuts him off:* It's Kurdistan. And it's important to see these things.

GEOFFREY: Poor baby. You're so sensitive and vulnerable.

PFENI: I'm fine.

GEOFFREY: There's nothing wrong with that, my darling. I've made a career out of being sensitive and vulnerable.

PFENI: Geoffrey . . .

GEOFFREY: What is it, Pfeni? What is it that you want, my angel, that you're not getting? Do you want to get married? We'll get married. Whenever you leave, I think to myself, "Why is she going again? Pfeni belongs here with me." You are the first person I want to see in the morning and the last person I want to talk to at night. Do you want to have children? Brill. We'll have a troop of them. They'll be running Metro-Goldwyn-Mayer before age seven.

PFENI: But will they be Jewish children?

GEOFFREY: They'll have to be if they're going to run M.G.M.

PFENI: Geoffrey, I'm already forty.

GEOFFREY: Time is on our side, angel. That's the joy of an unconventional life.

PFENI: Some days, Geoffrey, I wish I were you.

GEOFFREY: "Alas, our frailty is the cause, not we. For such as we are made of, such we be."

PFENI: Put on some pants, Geoffrey.

GEOFFREY: What?

PFENI: Just put on some pants.

GEOFFREY: You're much too modest.

PFENI: This is my sister's house.

GEOFFREY: And you think she's never seen a man without pants?

PFENI: She's never seen you without pants.

GEOFFREY: How do you know?

PFENI: Are you sure you're not part of some antifeminist, anti-Semitic plot?

GEOFFREY: What? You expect me to like women *and* Jews?

PFENI: God help me. "If I could only get to Moscow!"

GEOFFREY: I love being with you. Pfeni, what are you working on now?

PFENI: Right now? With you? Here this morning? In Sara's sitting room? Well, as we sit here, I have a new book about gender and class working in a crock pot somewhere in Tajikistan. It's writing itself.

GEOFFREY: You've been talking about that book for years. It's time to move on.

PFENI: I always move on. I'm a travel writer.

GEOFFREY: Pfeni, have you ever heard of a singer named Lilli Lehman?

PFENI: Was she a Marvellette or a Ronnette?

GEOFFREY: She was one of the greatest opera singers of all time.

PFENI: Oh well.

GEOFFREY: But by the time Lilli got around to making records, she was too old and her voice fairly shot. So what's the moral?

PFENI: Record early.

GEOFFREY: Pfeni, I am serious. I've changed address books three times this year because I couldn't bear to cross out any more names. I've lost too many friends. I've seen too many lights that never had their chance to glow burn out overnight. I've tried for years now to make sense of all this, and all I know is life is random and there is no case to be made for a just or loving god. So how then do we proceed? In directing terms, what is the objective? Of course, we must cherish those that we love. That's a given. But just as important, people like you and me have to work even harder to create the best art, the best theatre, the best bloody book about gender and class in Tajikistan that we possibly can. And the rest, the children, the country kitchen, the domestic bliss, we leave to others who will have different regrets. Pfeni, you and I can't idle time.

PFENI: I love you, Geoffrey. I'm not going to travel anymore. I want to stay with you.

———

Begins to take his hand as GORGEOUS *enters in a flannel nightgown.*

GORGEOUS: Hello. Hello.

GEOFFREY: Good morning!

GORGEOUS: Good morning! I thought I heard noises down here and I was hoping it meant it was time for coffee. Geoffrey, you have fabulous legs! *She hikes up her nightgown and puts her legs beside his.* I noticed because I happen to have great legs, too. Pfeni's ankles are good, but then she gets a little thick in the calves. *Grabs* GEOFFREY's *knee.* So, Geoffrey, Geoffrey, I can't tell you how excited my ladies were when I told them you agreed to have breakfast at the National with them this morning.

GEOFFREY, *confused:* I did? Brilliant.

GORGEOUS: Even Mrs. Hershkovitz with the Wedgwood said to me, "Well, well, Gorgeous, aren't you connected?" Everyone is always so impressed when I tell them about my sister who writes for the PLO and her famous director boyfriend.

PFENI: I don't write for the PLO. I did an interview with Hanan Ashrawi for my book four years ago.

GORGEOUS: She's a puppet for the PLO.

PFENI: She's a professor at Birzeit University.

GORGEOUS: Have it your way. Geoffrey honey, tell me about your new house. Is it almost finished?

GEOFFREY: Just another month. It's going to be marvelous. It has the most spectacular view of the Thames.

GORGEOUS: Uh-huh. So you and Pfeni will be moving there together soon?

PFENI: Gorgeous!

GORGEOUS: I tell my children that anything is possible if you just hold on to your dreams. You held on to your dreams, Geoffrey. All creative people do. That's why I'm so happy to have you in the family.

TESS, *offstage:* Mom, Mother, are you there? Have you seen my passport?

GORGEOUS: Tessie, darling. Don't come down here. Geoffrey has no clothes on.

GEOFFREY *gets up:* Well, I suppose I'd better go put on my face for Mrs. Hershkowitz.

GORGEOUS: Vitz. She's a Vitz.

GEOFFREY *kisses* PFENI: Good-bye, my darling. *Takes* GORGEOUS's *hand.* Gorgeous, I look forward to seeing you and your lovely ladies shortly. *Kisses* GORGEOUS's *hand.* GORGEOUS *curtsies. Then, as he exits, he mutters:* Vitz. She's a Vitz.

GORGEOUS: He really is so much fun! Well, they say companionship is 90% of any marriage. Even the best sex is gone in two years. And I know, because Henry and I had the most delicious sex!

PFENI: What are you doing?

GORGEOUS: What do you mean "What am I doing?" Pfeni, I came down for coffee. Your boyfriend was lounging in his Fruit of the Looms, and I was making pleasant morning conversation.

PFENI: And that's why you asked if we'll be moving in together next month?

GORGEOUS: Sweetsie, be happy I didn't ask about your sex life—about which I am dying to know. Tell me something, does Geoffrey still, you know, with men?

PFENI: You know, what, with men?

GORGEOUS: Pfeni, if you don't know by now, you're really in trouble.

PFENI: Gorgeous, we're living in the midst of a world health crisis!

GORGEOUS: I know that. But there are still safe ways to do it. Even in Newton.

PFENI: I love Geoffrey. As much as I've ever loved any man, and I've had my share. Is Geoffrey every Jewish mother's—never mind Jewish, make it Baptist, Buddhist, Bahai—dream date for their daughter? No, but Gorgeous, I'm not every mother's dream daughter.

GORGEOUS: Sweetsie, don't waste your time rebelling against mother anymore. She's not even here to enjoy it. It's just us now.

PFENI: I'm on deadline.

GORGEOUS: Ucch, sweetsie, why won't you take my advice. You're pretending to be someone you're not! Men, desirable men of any age, aren't interested in eccentric women in their forties. Eccentric women in their twenties is maybe interesting—especially with the big, funsy, way-out hair. Eccentric in their thirties is all right only if you're superthin and arty successful. But wandering around the world alone at forty, Pfeni, you're wandering yourself right out of the marketplace. And don't tell me you have Geoffrey. I know you can't judge a book by its cover, but sweetsie, you're at the wrong library altogether. Pfeni, don't you want what any normal woman wants?

PFENI: I never know what you mean by normal.

GORGEOUS: Pfeni, you and I are people people. We're not like Sara. We need warmth and cuddles and kisses.

PFENI: We sound like puppies.

GORGEOUS: Pfeni. Listen to your other smart big sister. You still have time. Don't waste it. *Strokes her cheek.* You know, your skin is very dry. You should have weekly collagen masks.

PFENI: I should?

GORGEOUS: And it's not too early for Retin A.

Enter TOM *and* TESS *from upstairs.*

TOM: Good morning, Aunt Pfeni. Good morning, Aunt Gorgeous.

GORGEOUS: Well, well, well. Teenagers, teenagers, teenagers.

TESS: Have you seen my Mom?

TOM: We saw her dancing last night with Mr. Mervyn, the furrier.

GORGEOUS: Well, well, well. I guess it was a full house.

TESS: He is a better choice for my mother than Benjamin Disraeli.

TOM: Who's Benjamin Disraeli?

GORGEOUS: A famous Jewish philanthropist. He founded Harrods department store.

PFENI *and* TESS *laugh with* GORGEOUS.

TESS: The furrier was singing Frank Sinatra.

GORGEOUS: Tessie, as your Aunt Pfeni can tell you, a good man is hard to find.

PFENI: Tessie, if my life depended on it, I would never tell you that.

Enter SARA.

SARA: Tell you what? Hello, my sisters. Hello, Tessie. *Goes to get the morning paper.*

TOM: Good morning, Mrs. Goode.

SARA: Good morning, Tom. This is an early family gathering. Have you all had your coffee?

TESS: Mother . . .

SARA: Yes, Tessie, my love.

TESS: Nothing.

GORGEOUS: Well, I'm not shy. How was it?

SARA: How was what?

GORGEOUS *winks:* How was your night?

SARA: Lovely. I spent it with my family and a few close friends. How was your night, Gorgeous?

GORGEOUS: We mean your night after the family and a few close friends.

SARA: Gorgeous, stop winking. You look like you have an astigmatism.

TESS: Mother, you slept with that furrier last night. Everyone here knows that.

SARA: I see.

GORGEOUS: We like him.

TOM: A good man is hard to find.

TESS: Aren't you happy?

GORGEOUS: This is so exciting, honey. I always said to mother, if only Sara would meet a furrier or a dentist.

SARA: Why not a C.P.A.? Gorgeous, I am not going to drive off into the sunset with a man I've had dinner with once.

GORGEOUS: Why not?

TESS: He's too nice?

GORGEOUS: Too warm? Where is he now?

SARA: Have you never heard of "privacy," "discretion"?

GORGEOUS: I just want to see you settled.

SARA: This is it, Gorgeous. Trust me, I'm settled.

GORGEOUS: Tessie, don't you want to see your mother settled with a nice man?

SARA: Gorgeous, you may be the happiest woman in all of Newton. You may even be healing the entire funsy Massachusetts Turnpike! But you are not our mother. Our mother is dead.

GORGEOUS: I am not a stupid woman, Sara!

SARA: Then explain to me why your mind is cluttered with nonsense.

GORGEOUS: Let me tell you something, Sara. Rabbi Pearlstein says you're very troubled because you never grew up to be the woman our mother expected us to be.

SARA: I beg your pardon?

GORGEOUS: Well, I'm sorry things have not worked out as you had hoped. But I can no longer allow you to hurt my feelings because you are so threatened by my pride in my husband, my family, and my accomplishments!

SARA: This is actually quite absurd!

GORGEOUS: Is it quite! Well, you can speak with your la-di-dah British accent, and Pfeni can send my children postcards from every ca-ca-mamie capital in the world, but I know that deep inside both of you wish you were me! Dr. Gorgeous Teitelbaum, a middle-aged West Newton housewife who wears imitation Ferragamo shoes and is very soon to have her own cable call-in talk show! *She trips as she exits.* God damn it! I wish I had a pair of real friggin' Manulo Blahnik, Blanchik, fuck-it shoes! Pardon my French, Tom. *Exits upstairs.*

TOM: That wasn't French, Mrs. Goode.

SARA: Thank you, Tom.

TESS: Mother, we were all having such a nice time down here. We were all so happy for you, and then you came down and spoiled it.

SARA: Well, this is my house.

TESS: Yes, it is. Where do you keep my passport? We're leaving for Vilnius tomorrow morning.

TOM: We want to get there in time for independence.

SARA: Tessie, can we please talk about this quietly after breakfast?

TESS: "Quietly after breakfast" means without Tom. Tom and I are here together.

SARA: Yes, I see. Pfeni, do you have nothing to add to your niece flying off tomorrow?

TESS: Aunt Pfeni flies all over the world.

SARA: But for a reason. You have no bloody reason to fly off to Vilnius during a revolution!

TESS: Let's go, Tom. Just because it's not important to her to have any passion in her life doesn't mean that we can't. *Exits.*

SARA *calls after her:* Don't call me "her," Tessie.

TOM: Mrs. Goode, me mum and me sisters don't get on all the time either. There are twelve of them and good Roman Catholics, Mrs. Goode.

SARA: That's nice.

TOM: Have a nice day, Mrs. Goode. Me dad sings Frank Sinatra too. *Exits.*

SARA: Why couldn't she take up with a lovely boy from the IRA? At least it's close by.

PFENI: Sara, I just want to know one thing.

SARA: What?

PFENI: How was it?

SARA: Oh! How was it? Well, I'd say that furrier has some very special skills.

PFENI: Really! You mean, like synthetic animal covering?

SARA *laughs:* Let's just call it "fun fur."

PFENI: What?

SARA: When you're older.

PFENI: Do you think Gorgeous and Henry have "the most delicious sex"? She's always talking about it.

SARA: Maybe Gorgeous is the smartest one of us all. Maybe if I were "settled," my daughter wouldn't be on the road to being a new-age Emma Goldman.

PFENI: You don't believe that.

SARA: Not for a minute. Please talk to Tessie today. It frightens me how much she's like you.

PFENI: How can I tell Tessie not to go to Vilnius when I was up all last night watching Kurdish refugee evacuations? In some crazy way I wished I could be there.

SARA: But unlike my daughter you're a grown person and a journalist. Why don't you go?

PFENI: I don't do that kind of writing anymore.

SARA: Why not?

PFENI: Don't know. I won't. I don't. Who knows?

SARA: That's a succinct and thoughtful answer.

PFENI: Sara, I had the most unsettling experience last week. Before Bombay I went back to Doubandi, my Afghan village. I wanted to visit the women I'd written about, but when I arrived, I was told that half of them were dead and the rest refugees. And Sara, with every bit of dire information, I became more and more excited to listen.

SARA: I don't understand.

PFENI: Somewhere I need the hardship of the Afghan women and the Kurdish suffering to fill up my life for me. And if I'm that empty, then I might as well continue to wander to the best hotels, restaurants, and poori stands.

SARA: But how are you helping them if you don't tell their stories? Is it morally better to dispatch four-star Karachi hotel reviews?

PFENI: It's wrong for me to use these women.

SARA: Pfeni, real compassion is genuinely rarer than any correct agenda. I'm a pretty good banker, but it's not a passion. You, on the other hand, have a true calling, and the sad and surprisingly weak thing is you're actively trying to avoid it. I think you care too much and you're looking for excuses not to. Tessie says I should have a talk show instead of Gorgeous. "Opinions with Sara Goode." *Returns to reading the paper.*

PFENI *takes* SARA'S *hand:* There is no one I rely on in life more than you. There is no one I am more grateful to than you.

SARA, *moving her hand away:* Pfeni, don't, and I won't.

Enter MERV, *humming "Just the Way You Look Tonight."*

MERV: Good morning.

PFENI: Good morning, Merv. How nice to see you again. I'm afraid I have a deadline.

SARA: I thought you finished "Bombay by Night."

PFENI: Yes, now there's "Bombay by Day." *Exits downstairs.*

MERV: She is a hard-working girl, your sister.

SARA: We're all hard-working girls. So, what's on your agenda?

MERV: My agenda?

SARA, *British:* Your schedule.

MERV: I love the way you say schedule. Say "vitamin."

SARA, *British:* Vitamin.

MERV: Again.

SARA, *giggling:* Vitamin.

MERV: That's adorable. *Kisses her.*

SARA: I have a tennis date this morning. And you?

MERV: Me? I don't have a tennis date this morning.

SARA: I'm just being reasonably clear.

MERV: Isn't it usually the reverse? Aren't most women warm and cozy the morning after and the men reasonably clear?

SARA: I wouldn't know.

MERV: I've never met anyone like you, Sara. You're warm and cold all at the same time. Your face is so familiar and so distant. Sometimes I look at you and see all my mother's photographs of her mother and her mother's entire family.

SARA: Well, it's a look.

MERV: My mother's family had a villa in a spa resort in Poland called Ciechocinek. And the pictures we had were of the family gathered at a picnic. The men waving at the camera or smiling, holding up a cantaloupe! They were sweet, these men, some even handsome, but they couldn't hold a candle to the women. The women in their too-large dresses with their arms folded all had your brilliant eyes—they sparkled even from those curled and faded photographs. Unfortunately, most of them and their families didn't survive. But Sara, when I look into your eyes, I see those women's strength and their intelligence. To me you are a beautiful and most remarkable woman. Why are you laughing? You're like a teenager. I say you're beautiful and you start laughing?

SARA: You want to hear something cuckoo, Merv?

MERV: You cuckoo? You're too "not cuckoo" for your own good.

SARA: I've been to Ciechocinek. I was sent there by the Hong Kong/Shanghai Bank.

MERV: My mother always said it was the Palm Beach of Poland.

SARA: It's now a postmodern, prefab, post-cold-war resort of the gray cinder block variety.

MERV: Thank God there's somewhere for me to retire besides Coral Gables. Sadie . . . *Begins laughing.* Why did the Hong Kong Shanghainese send you to Ciechocinek? Never in my life did I think I'd be asking a woman such a question!

SARA: Someone has to pay to privatize the state industries. Capitalism is expensive, Merv. They were asking for a loan, and I was being reasonably clear.

MERV: I'm sure you were brilliant.

SARA: I was all right. But while I reviewed their detailed proposals for renovating heating services and redistricting agricultural cooperatives, I couldn't help but see it all as a minor triumph for the women with those same sparkling eyes in my mother's faded photographs. Fifty years after the lucky few had escaped with false passports, Esther Malchah's granddaughter Sara was deciding how to put bread on the tables of those who had so blithely driven them all away.

MERV: I want to know you better, Sara. We could spend some pleasant time together. You can meet my children, and I already like Tessie. We're not young, Sara.

SARA: And a good man is hard to find. Mervyn . . .

MERV: "Mervyn." That means you're pulling away again.

SARA: I think you've set your sights on the wrong sister.

MERV: Do you make a practice of spending the night with men you plan to fix up with your sisters?

SARA: I think you and someone like Gorgeous could be quite happy together. You're both very lively.

MERV: What does that mean?

SARA: You have interests in common.

MERV: You mean we're both a little too lively and a little

too Jewish. That's what we have in common. Sara, you remind me of my classmates from DeWitt Clinton High School in the Bronx who now pretend as if DeWitt Clinton was a prep school down the Connecticut River right around the bend from Groton or St. Paul's.

SARA: St. Paul's is in New Hampshire and Groton School is in Massachusetts. Groton, Connecticut is a shipbuilding town.

MERV: You would know that.

SARA: I don't see what any of this has to do with you and someone like Gorgeous.

MERV: I'm afraid that you do, or you wouldn't be chasing Lord Gefilte, and Gorgeous and I wouldn't be quite so happy together. I don't understand what's so wrong with you, Sara. I like you.

SARA: Your world is very different from mine.

MERV: No, it's not. I changed my name from Kantlowitz, and my daughter, the Israeli captain, went to St. Paul's. And where did you come from, Sara?

SARA: Don't proselytize me, Merv.

MERV: Sara, you're an American Jewish woman living in London, working for a Chinese Hong Kong bank, and taking weekends at a Polish resort with a daughter who's running off to Lithuania!

SARA: And who are you? My knight in shining armor? The furrier who came to dinner. Why won't you give up, Merv? I'm a cold, bitter woman who's turned her back on her family, her religion, and her country! And I held so much in. I harbored so much guilt that it all made me ill and capsized in my ovaries. Isn't that the way the old assimilated story goes?

MERV: Why do you dislike me so much?

SARA: I don't dislike you, Merv.

MERV: Then what is your problem, lady?

SARA: "Lady," that's very Brooklyn.

MERV: No, actually, it's very the Bronx. Is it because I remind you too much of home?

SARA: Merv, the home you're talking about is the Bronx, the Brooklyn, the America of forty years ago. It doesn't even exist anymore.

MERV: If it doesn't exist, why the hell are you working so hard to make it go away?

SARA: I didn't have a "you" in my life at sixteen. I'm certainly not going to have a "you" in my life now. You deserve someone who really does know how to throw a good Shabbes. Someone who will make you a "warm and happy home" and show up at holidays and family gatherings in a tasteful but cheery crepe orange suit.

MERV: And you can't, Sara Rosensweig?

SARA: You don't know me as well as you think you do. Orange pales my already far too sallow skin.

MERV *extends his hand:* It was a pleasure to meet you, Sara.

SARA *holds onto his hand:* You're a very nice man.

MERV: Do women like it when a man says, "I'm sorry. You're very nice"?

SARA: No. Especially not when the man has just spent the night.

MERV: You still have all the answers, Sara. *Exits.*

SARA *goes to the record player and puts away the Sinatra album. She picks up the Cliffe Clef album and puts it on the record player when the phone rings. She picks up the phone.*

SARA: Oh, hello, Nick. Yes, it was a lovely evening. Glynebourne Tuesday would be terrific. Oh, I'm so sorry. Your gift was absolutely brilliant. And Tessie thought it was brilliant as well. Thanks so much. See you Tuesday. Good-bye.

She turns on the record player and picks up a gift box that has remained unwrapped on the window seat. As she sits to open the gift, we hear on the record, "Hi, I'm Sara Rosensweig of Brooklyn, New York and we're the Cliffe Clef of 1959." There are assorted cheers. "Tonight is our concert of Europe." There are assorted laughs. SARA *laughs and shrugs her shoulders.* "Well, we call it that as a tribute to Metternich, Talleyrand, and other well-known Harvard men." *There are more laughs.* "Those of us who are graduating this year . . ." *There is a whooping cheer, and* SARA *raises her arm in triumph.* "Each has a chance tonight to lead with her favorite song, and this one, ever since freshman year, has been mine." *The group begins to sing a cappella* "MacNamara's Band." SARA *listens. She continues to unwrap the gift. Suddenly she begins to sing a different verse softly:*

> Oh my name is Moishe Pupick
> And I come from Palestine,
> I live on bread and honey
> And on Manischewitz wine.
> Oh my mother makes the best
> Gefilte fish in all the land . . .

Her voice cracks.

> And I'm the only Yiddish girl
> In MacNamara's Band.

SARA *is crying as she lifts up a standard tea kettle from the gift box.* It's brilliant, Nick. Absolutely fucking brilliant.

Scene 2

Later that afternoon, around 4:00 P.M. PFENI *enters from downstairs, with her laptop computer. She sits on the window seat and works.* TESS *enters carrying a tray with tea cups and a pot of tea. The final bars of the Cliffe Clefs' singing "When My Sugar Walks Down the Street" is on the stereo.*

TESS: Your tea, madam.

PFENI: Thank you, Tessie. I rely on the kindness of nieces.

TESS: Are you writing something new?

PFENI: I have an idea. And that's a very good thing.

Enter GEOFFREY.

GEOFFREY: I've returned from the Crimea, my darling, and I've missed you so! Could this be little Tessie? Let me look at you. You've grown into a beautiful woman. Oh God, I'm old! How old do I look to you today, Tessie?

TESS: Mmmmm. About seventy.

GEOFFREY: She's a nasty little thing, isn't she? No more ginger cookies for you, young lady.

TESS: I'm going upstairs to pack.

GEOFFREY: Are you really off to the Baltics, then?

TESS: Yes! There's a rally here tonight, and Tom says we'll leave tomorrow. *She runs up the stairs singing:*

All the little birdies go tweet-tweet-tweet!

GEOFFREY: I'm thinking of making a film, *Three Days That Shook the Rosensweigs,* with Dr. Gorgeous making her film debut as Trotsky.

PFENI: I sort of envy Tessie going.

GEOFFREY: But my darling, she's not going anywhere. Trust me, Pfeni, I have an eye for real talent.

PFENI: You're such a bloody snob!

GEOFFREY: Perhaps I was once. But not anymore. I've had my consciousness raised by the full assemblage of the Temple Beth El sisterhood.

PFENI *kisses him:* I take it all back, you're not a snob. You're a saint.

GEOFFREY: I fielded such penetrating questions from Mrs. Ida Hershkovitz as, "Mr. Duncan, I would like to know what exactly your function as director of *The Scarlet Pimpernel* was. You didn't write the story or the music and you don't act. So, from my point of view, you're being paid very good money just to sit there and do nothing."

PFENI: Poor Gorgeous.

GEOFFREY: Gorgeous loves it, darling! She's a star! The most beautiful and well-connected woman in Newton. They've asked me to the States to direct the West Newton Community Center revival of *Milk and Honey.* I suggested we do *Marat/Sade* instead. *Kisses her.* I love that you have no bloody idea what I'm babbling about. Did Jordan ring? He said he'd be by around now.

PFENI: No, he didn't ring. Was Jordan at your talk?

GEOFFREY: I thought the ladies might want to meet him. Royal Jordan flatware is very big in the States these days. *Takes a sip of Pfeni's tea and spits it out into the cup.* What's the matter with this tea? Ucccch! Undrinkable!

PFENI: Geoffrey, that was mine!

GEOFFREY: "I would give all my fame for a pot of ale and safety."

PFENI: Geoffrey, please sit down. You're making me anxious.

GEOFFREY *sings and dances:*

> Oh pretty baby, I can't sit down.
> Don't you hear the band a groovin', I can't sit down.
> Gotta get your motor movin'.

All right, U.S., for fifty points?

PFENI: "You Can't Sit Down," 1963. The Dovelles.

GEOFFREY: You're the brightest woman I've ever known.

PFENI: No, my sister Sara's the brightest woman you've ever known.

GEOFFREY *finally sits:* Pfeni . . .

PFENI: What is it, Geoffrey? You're beyond manic today.

GEOFFREY: Pfeni, after my speech to the Gorgeous ladies, I drove around London for hours. And then up past the Isle of Dogs and out to Greenwich. And I sat at the water's edge on the bow of the Cutty Sark and thought about us. Mostly about you, actually. Pfeni, I love you. I will always love you. But the truth is, I miss men. What?

PFENI: Nothing.

GEOFFREY: I want us to be the most remarkable friends. The Noel and Gertie of our day.

PFENI: I'm not in the theatre, Geoffrey. I'm a journalist.

GEOFFREY: You know how wonderful I think you are. You must know that the entire time I've been with you, I've never acted out, I've never cheated on you.

PFENI: Really, not even on the Cutty Sark?

GEOFFREY: Bitchiness doesn't become you, darling.

PFENI: I'm sorry.

GEOFFREY: You also don't have to be so bloody polite.

PFENI: The only place I am at home, or even close, is when I'm with you.

GEOFFREY: Pfeni, when I sat next to you at the ballet, it was a dark time in my life. Jordan had just left me, and my friends were becoming increasingly ill.

PFENI: So you thought to yourself, why not try something completely different. Why not get as far away from the hurt and the fear as possible. And there I was seated beside you; pretty, eccentric, and more than just a little bit lonely. You're right. You do have an eye for real talent!

GEOFFREY: Pfeni, don't.

PFENI: Why? Am I being self-indulgent? And maybe even just a little bitchy? Geoffrey, you're the one who said we should get married that very first night. You're the one who said, what beautiful children we'd have just this morning.

GEOFFREY: But we would have beautiful children. Pfeni, my friends need me.

PFENI: I never stopped you from being there for them.

GEOFFREY: I was frightened.

PFENI: And you're not now?

Pause.

GEOFFREY: You really don't understand what it is to have absolutely no idea who you are.

PFENI: What?

GEOFFREY: I thought about this on the bow of the clipper ship. For all your wandering, you're always basically the same—you have your sisters, your point of view, and even in some casual drop-in way, your God. Pfeni, the only time I have a real sense of who I am and where I'm going is when I'm in a darkened theatre and we're making it all up. Starting from scratch. But now I want a real life outside the theatre, too. So maybe I will regret this choice. I know I'll miss you. But I'm an instinctive person, my luv, and speaking to those ladies, it all just clicked. Today this is who I am. I have no other choice. I miss men.

PFENI: It's all right, Geoffrey, I do too. *A car horn is heard.* Jordan.

GEOFFREY: I don't have to go.

PFENI: He's waiting for you.

GEOFFREY: We're in no rush.

PFENI: Please, Geoffrey, just go.

GEOFFREY *kisses her head:* Sugar pie, honey bunch.

Enter SARA *in a tennis outfit.*

SARA: Jordan's outside, Geoffrey. He's looking rather well. He's driving a red Miata convertible. Things must be booming in the flatware design business. I suggested he move into cups and saucers, and we'll all get into business. Pfeni can be in charge of worldwide distribution, Geoffrey, you'll be director of special events, and Jordan

can introduce his new line of sheets on Gorgeous's talk
show. There, I've solved all of our futures!

GEOFFREY: The thing that no one can appreciate about you,
Sara, is you're remarkably sweet. *The horn honks again.*
I think I have a crush on all the sisters Rosensweig. *Exits.*

SARA: Maybe he just likes Jewish girls. Do you think I'm too
old for a red convertible? Jordan says it works for any
age.

PFENI: That's nice.

SARA: What's nice?

PFENI: Whatever Jordan said.

SARA: I thought you never particularly cared for him.

PFENI: He's fine. It's people I don't like very much, Sara.

SARA: Why are you always so hard on yourself? Oh God,
it's raining again. I hope Jordan puts his top up.

PFENI: Geoffrey misses men.

SARA: What?

PFENI: Geoffrey just took a drive to the Isle of Dogs and he
realized he misses men.

SARA: My poor baby sister.

PFENI: I really don't like people, Sara.

SARA: Pfeni, you're a beautiful and brilliant woman. Next
time just don't agree to marry the man you're sitting
next to at *Giselle*. See *Swan Lake* instead. C'mon, luvey,
have a cup of tea.

PFENI: I need a Brioschi.

SARA: What?

PFENI *sings softly:* "Eat too much, drink too much, take
Brioschi, take Brioschi!" Named, I'm sure, for the eminent Dr. Brioschi. One night, when I was around nine, I
was watching Rosemary Clooney on "Your Hit Parade"
with our mother in Brooklyn. Rosemary was singing some

sad love song, and I asked mother what a broken heart felt like. She thought I meant heartburn and told me when I grew up to take Brioschi.

SARA: How do you remember these things?

PFENI: How could I forget? Sara, I don't want to lose Geoffrey and Mommy at the same time. And they don't even make Brioschi anymore!

SARA *embraces* PFENI *as* PFENI *begins to cry:* Yes they do. Shah, Penny, shah!

GORGEOUS *enters, drenched, with an umbrella and a shopping bag. She is wearing only one shoe.*

GORGEOUS: Does it ever stop raining in this country? A person could drown just from walking.

SARA: It was beautiful just a minute ago.

GORGEOUS: That's what's even worse. You never know where you stand. *She gives a Wedgwood gift to* SARA. This is for you, Sara. Thank you very much. I had a lovely stay. I'll just go upstairs and pack my things and be gone in an hour. Mrs. Hershkovitz said I could room with her tonight. Pfeni, if you leave for Bora Bora or Karachi before I come back down, it was great to see you, sweetsie. Your boyfriend was terrific with the ladies this morning. Hold on to him, honey. He's a gem. *Begins going up the stairs.*

SARA: Gorgeous?

GORGEOUS: Yes, Sara.

SARA: What happened to your shoe?

GORGEOUS: What shoe? *Pulls a heel out of her bag.* You call this a shoe? It's a heel. A four-hundred-dollar, imported from Italy, genuine all man-made material goddamned heel!

SARA: Gorgeous, sit down. Have some tea.

GORGEOUS: I'd rather stand. Rabbi Pearlstein says I should finish the tour and come home.

PFENI: You called him?

GORGEOUS: Let me tell you that, thanks to both of you, this has not been an especially enjoyable trip for me. I've spent two days schlepping around London with the sisterhood and two nights having my own sisters tell me everything I do is wrong. Then I decide to treat myself to a little something because I can't bear the stress anymore.

SARA: Gorgeous, I'm—

GORGEOUS: Let me finish. So I go to eight shoe stores on Sloane Street—one nicer than the other. I spread my toes in Tanino Crisci, I slide into the Ferragamos with the bows, and I even clip-clop in royal velvet Manulo Blanchiki frontless, backless mules. And finally, I make my choice—an exquisite pair I know I've seen before on the feet of Fergie or Di or Lady Michael of Kent. They're the softest grosgrain, on the shapeliest heel I've ever seen. I take out my charge card—with tax it comes to two hundred pounds—that's four hundred dollars for a pair of shoes—don't tell me that's insane, I know, but I'm tired and I decide for once I'm worth it.

SARA: Of course!

GORGEOUS: I'm not finished! So I'm walking past Harrods in my new shoes, and for the first time since I arrived here I feel like a person. I debate taking the taxi back to Queen Anne's Gate, and I decide that just because I have shoes like Princess Di, I shouldn't spend like her. So I go into the tube stop at Kensington Station. I get on the escalator, and guess what happens—the shapely goddamned heel gets caught and rips the hell out of my four-hundred-dollar shoe! And all along a blind man with a cup is watching me. And I think to myself, I'm being punished by God because I did not give that man money, even if he is a fake!

SARA: Let me see your shoe, Gorgeous. I have a brilliant cobbler.

GORGEOUS: Sara, even the Sir Isaac Newton of footwear couldn't fix these!

SARA: Let me see it.

GORGEOUS: Sara, there are things in life that you do not have the answers to and one of them is my shoes. *She pulls the remaining pump from her bag.* They are shot, hopeless, kaplooie! *Throws the shoe into the coal bin.*

SARA: Henry will buy you another pair of shoes. I'll call and tell him the brand. *Reaches for the phone.*

GORGEOUS: Put the phone down, Sara.

SARA: Henry will listen to me. What are big sisters for?

GORGEOUS: Henry can't buy me or anyone else in his family a pair of shoes. My dear husband Henry hasn't worked in two years.

SARA: That's ridiculous. He's a lawyer.

GORGEOUS: As a banker there's something going on that you should know about, Sara. It's called a recession.

SARA: But Henry's a Harvard lawyer.

GORGEOUS: And I'm Dr. Gorgeous. Pish-pish.

SARA: I thought he was a partner.

GORGEOUS: Sara, my banker genius sister, the partnership was dissolved.

PFENI: But something will obviously turn up.

GORGEOUS: Sweetsie, they can get someone young and peppy for half the price. I'm going upstairs to pack. I need to rest and go home.

SARA: Maybe I know someone.

GORGEOUS: You don't know anybody! Henry isn't even looking for a job. He's writing mysteries in the basement.

SARA: What?

GORGEOUS: He says he could have been Raymond Chandler or Dashiell Hammett if only he hadn't been brought up in Scarsdale. So now every night at ten he dresses in a trench coat and goes out to prowl around the bars of South End. He comes home at five in the morning and begins typing in the basement until he falls asleep at noon. We pass each other in the hall and he tells me how much it means to him that I am still here. And you know the funniest part of it all? He doesn't even drink. He's out all night having diet Cokes.

SARA: He should see a psychiatrist.

GORGEOUS: I am a psychiatrist.

SARA: You're a lay analyst.

GORGEOUS: Pish-pish. They don't know any more than I do. Stick with Geoffrey, Pfeni. He's handsome, he's rich, and who cares about sex, it goes away after six months anyway. All the ladies fell in love with Geoffrey. Mrs. Hershkovitz thought he was so adorable, she sent over this genuine Wedgwood chachka for him. It cost about as much as my shoes.

SARA: I thought it was for me.

GORGEOUS: Mrs. Hershkovitz sent it over for both of you. Where is Geoffrey?

SARA: He went away for the weekend with Jordan.

PFENI: Geoffrey met Mrs. Hershkovitz and realized he missed men.

GORGEOUS: Sweetsie, don't take it personally.

PFENI: I am so stupid.

GORGEOUS: Sara, tell her none of Rita Rosensweig's daughters are stupid.

SARA: Is stupid. Merv, the world leader in leopardette, isn't here anymore either. I was big and mean and nasty and chased him far away.

GORGEOUS: Why did you do that?

SARA: I don't know, Gorgeous. You just told me there are things in life that I don't have the answers to.

GORGEOUS: Well, did you like him?

SARA: Actually, I had a nice time.

GORGEOUS: Did you tell him that?

SARA: No. I told him he was a very nice man instead.

GORGEOUS & PFENI *sigh:* Ugh.

GORGEOUS: How did our nice Jewish mother do such a lousy job on us?

SARA: Why is it her fault? She always told me to say thank you, I had a lovely time.

GORGEOUS: Well, it's not Daddy's fault. He called me Gorgeous.

PFENI, *getting up:* Personally, I feel that tea time is over. And we can now move right into wine.

SARA: Such a good baby sister.

GORGEOUS: Very good. And gifted.

PFENI *takes a bottle from the wine rack:* This cab-sauv has a reputation for being rather versatile.

GORGEOUS: Pish-pish.

SARA *giggles:* Double pish-pish.

PFENI *pours them all wine:* What does pish-pish actually mean?

SARA: Gorgeous, have you met my sister the wandering gentile?

GORGEOUS: Pfeni, when Geoffrey told you he missed men, what did you do?

PFENI: I said I missed them, too.

They laugh.

GORGEOUS: Good girl!

SARA: Brilliant girl! Maybe Rita Rosensweig didn't do so badly by us after all.

PFENI *lifts her glass:* To Rita!

GORGEOUS *lifts her glass:* To Rita!

SARA *lifts her glass:* To Rita! And her stunningly brilliant daughters.

GORGEOUS & PFENI: And her stunningly brilliant daughters. *They sip the wine.* Mmmmm, versatile.

GORGEOUS *sits:* Drinking goes directly to my feet. Does it go to your feet, Pfeni?

PFENI: No, my head. Directly to my head. What about you, Sara?

SARA *sits:* In my hair. I feel it in my hair.

GORGEOUS: I'm exhausted.

PFENI: Me too. Very tired.

They both lie down on SARA. Sara strokes their foreheads.

GORGEOUS: Sara, didn't Mama always say you were a shtarker? Maybe you should take care of us now.

PFENI: That would be very nice.

GORGEOUS: Pfeni, do you know what a shtarker is?

PFENI: A person who takes charge. A general in the Cossack army.

SARA: That must be why I'm so popular!

GORGEOUS *kisses* SARA's *hand.*

GORGEOUS: You have nice hands, Sara. But you should use hot oil treatments. It would loosen your cuticles. What do you think, Pfeni?

PFENI: I think Sara was a starker to that nice Merlin.

SARA: Shtarker. But I really hardly even know him.

GORGEOUS: You could get to know him. Call him.

GORGEOUS & PFENI, *chanting:* Call him! Call him! Call him!

SARA: Please. Girls, girls, girls. *She holds both their faces in her hands.* My two little sisters! Gorgeous and also Gorgeous. We are—

ALL THREE: The sisters Gorgeous! *They laugh.*

GORGEOUS: You know what I wish with all my heart?

SARA: What?

PFENI: What?

GORGEOUS: I wish that on one of our birthdays, when all the children and men have gone upstairs to sleep . . .

SARA: What men?

GORGEOUS: And we finally sit together, just us three sisters . . .

PFENI: Around the samovar.

GORGEOUS: And we talk about life!

PFENI: And art.

SARA: Pfeni!

GORGEOUS: Thank you, Sara. *Kisses* SARA's *hand.* That each of us can say at some point that we had a moment of pure, unadulterated happiness! Do you think that's possible, Sara?

SARA: Brief. But a moment or two.

PFENI: I like that.

GORGEOUS: Me too.

"That each of us can say at some point that we had a moment of pure, unadulterated happiness!" (Madeline Kahn, Jane Alexander, Francis McDormand) © 1992 Martha Swope

Pause.

SARA: Gorgeous, there's something I've been meaning to share
    with you.
GORGEOUS: What?
SARA: Your neck is very dry.
GORGEOUS: No.
SARA: Don't you think her neck is dry, Pfeni?
PFENI: Let me see. *Touches her.* Oh, yes, very dry!
SARA: Don't you think she should use that special rejuvena-
    tion treatment? The deluxe pish-pish one!
PFENI: Oh, that pish-pish rejuvenation treatment! Yes, I think
    so. *They both suddenly jump on* GORGEOUS *and begin
    tickling her.* Rabbi Pearlstein says more collagen shots!
GORGEOUS: No! No! Pfeni, stop and you can have my re-
    maining shoe! *Jumps up from the sofa.*
PFENI: I want that shoe. Gorgeous, gimme that shoe! Gor-
    geous! *Chases* GORGEOUS *upstairs. They are laughing and
    giggling like children.* Gorgeous!

SARA *remains on the couch, listening and smiling.*

S CENE 3

*Early Sunday morning. The Clefs singing "And a Nightingale Sang." *TOM *and* TESS *come downstairs. They hug, and* TOM *leaves with his bag.* TESS *begins listening to the music. She speaks into her tape recorder.*

TESS: What exactly did the nightingale sing in Berkeley Square? And why not in Hyde Park or Hampstead Heath?

GORGEOUS *enters in an aerobic ensemble.*

GORGEOUS: Hello! Hello! I just finished my morning exercises and I thought I heard activity. Tessie, why don't you listen to more contemporary music? I'll loan you my exercise tapes.

TESS: I'm finishing my summer project. Do you mind if I interview you?

GORGEOUS: Of course.

TESS: Your name is?

GORGEOUS: My name is Dr. Gorgeous Teitelbaum. I am a housewife, mother, and radio personality.

TESS: Tell me about my mother as a girl.

GORGEOUS: Your mother never had a sense of style. Her dolls were always half-naked and mine were perfectly groomed. In fact, I was the one who taught your mother how to pull herself together. I gave her my prescription to dress for success.

TESS: What was that?

GORGEOUS: Accessories!

TESS: What?

GORGEOUS: Accessories are the key to fashion. Tessie, honey, you can wear real junk from Filene's basement, but with the right earrings, bracelet, and scarf you will always be very "too-too." You go into my closet today, pull together an ensemble, practice around the house, and let me check it. That's how I taught my own daughters, and they thanked me for it.

Enter PFENI *carrying her shopping bags and computer.*

TESS: Are you leaving now, Aunt Pfeni?

PFENI: Are you, Niece Tess? Aren't you supposed to be on the road to Vilnius?

TESS: Well, I went with Tom to the rally last night, and everyone was holding hands and singing Lithuanian folk songs. But the more they smiled at me and held my hand, the more apart from it all I became. Aunt Pfeni, are we people who will always be watching and never belong?

PFENI: How did you get to be so young and intelligent?

GORGEOUS: Where are you going now, sweetsie?

PFENI: Back to work. I'm going to a crock pot in Tajikistan.

GORGEOUS: Why did you choose that? I can't even spell it.

PFENI: Well, Gorgeous, if you only write "Bombay by Night" and you make sure to fall in love with men who can never really love you back, one morning you wake up at forty in your big sister's house, and where you should be seems sort of clear. *Kisses Gorgeous.* Good-bye, Gorgeous.

GORGEOUS: Sunblock, sweetsie.

TESS: But Aunt Pfeni, what if I need you?

PFENI: The best life advice I've ever gotten was from your mother, and the best moisturizer was from your aunt. So the way I see it, they can cover the entire temporal and spiritual world. *She embraces* TESS. Tessie, I'll see you soon.

TESS: When is that?

PFENI: Soon is soon.

The doorbell rings.

GORGEOUS: There's always activity in this house.

PFENI *opens the door.*

MERV *enters, carrying a large box:* Good morning, ladies.

GORGEOUS: Merlin!

MERV: This is such a family of early risers! I'm sorry I can't stay. I have a car waiting outside.

GORGEOUS: Sit down, Merlin, relax, the car knows how to wait. Let Tessie bring you some of Sara's fabulous homemade oatmeal.

MERV: To tell you the truth, I only came because I got a message from Sara that I left my shirt. She said she'd put it by the door.

PFENI: Sara called you!

GORGEOUS: Tessie, get the oatmeal! I know there's something in that box Merlin is carrying and it's bigger than a bread box and furrier than a bear, and he's just waiting for us all to leave so that he can give it to Sara. *Calls.* Sara!!

MERV: It's for you, actually.

GORGEOUS: For me!

MERV *looks at the note:* It says, "For Gorgeous, with love." It was outside on the steps when I arrived.

GORGEOUS: It's from Mrs. Hershkovitz and the sisterhood. "Dearest Gorgeous, no one works harder than you. Isn't it time you had the real thing? Thank you for a job beautifully done." *Opens the box and immediately clutches her heart.* Oh my God! Oh my God! Hold me, Tessie.

PFENI: Tessie, hold your Aunt Gorgeous.

GORGEOUS *pulls a Chanel suit out of the box.*

GORGEOUS: It's the real thing! A genuine Chanel suit! And a purse! and earrings! And even the shoes! They got me the shoes! *She immediately pulls off her aerobic shoes and puts on the Chanels.* The classic pump! 7AA. How did they know 7AA? They're so comfortable! Am I floating! *Walks around the room.* I swear I'm floating. Tessie, pass me the skirt. Merlin, you're a furrier, drape me the scarf. *Puts on the skirt and the jacket over her aerobic gear.*

MERV: This is quality goods! I'm glad they didn't send the ones they sell on the street.

GORGEOUS: I haven't been so happy since the day I found out I made cheerleader and I knew that Sara didn't. *Poses in the full ensemble.* Do I look like Audrey Hepburn? I swear I feel just like Audrey Hepburn.

MERV: You look Gorgeous!

PFENI: Beyond Gorgeous!

GORGEOUS: I need the earrings. *Puts them on.* I am going right now to Claridge's to show Mrs. Hershkovitz and the ladies.

TESS: Right now?

GORGEOUS: Yes, and then I'm going directly to the House of Chanel to return every last piece of this.

PFENI: What?

GORGEOUS: Sweetsie, somebody's got to pay for tuition this fall, and better Chanel than Henry or me. Tessie, put my sneakers and purse in that box. I'll let your Aunt Pfeni drop me off and I'll jog home just for funsy. I wish they sent blue instead of pink, because blue is not my color. Pfeni, we'd better hurry or I'll lose my will power. It's very hard for me to postpone gratification. If I have something in my hand for more than two minutes, I want to keep it or at least eat it. Merlin, I hope you've moved in by the time I get back. *Exits with the box.*

PFENI *calls upstairs:* Sara! Sara! I'm leaving.

TESS: I wish Aunt Gorgeous could keep just the earrings.

PFENI: Sara!!

TESS: Mother!! SARA *comes down.* Mother, look who's here!

SARA: Hello Merv.

MERV: Hello Sara.

PFENI: Tally-ho, Sir Murf! Good-bye, my big sister.

SARA *touches* PFENI's *face:* I'll miss you.

PFENI: I'm a wandering Jew, Sara. I'll see you soon. *Exits.*

MERV: Sara, can I have my shirt? I've got a lunch date with the rabbi of Dublin.

SARA: Mervyn, you came all the way to Queen Anne's Gate. Please sit a minute.

TESS: Sit down, Merv. I'll get your shirt. *Winks at her mother.*

SARA: Tessie, you've caught your aunt's astigmatism. TESS *runs upstairs.* Would you like a drink?

MERV: Sara, it's eight o'clock in the morning.

SARA: How 'bout a little cassoulet?

MERV: What's on your mind, Sara?

SARA: Do you know how many cabbage rose bouquets are on this wallpaper? Forty-six.

MERV: You had me come all the way to Queen Anne's Gate to tell me this. Sara, I'm a grown man with a plane to catch and you're a very mature and responsible woman. What is it that you want?

SARA: I don't like that "very mature."

MERV: All right. You're a "stunning grownup."

SARA: Merv, I spent yesterday afternoon from teatime until sundown on this sofa counting the roses on the wall and waiting for you to call. And I have to tell you I'm furious with you for putting me in that position.

MERV: But how would I have known you wanted me to call?

SARA: From my very consistently warm and welcoming behavior. Merv, there's nothing I look forward to more on Saturday nights than getting into bed early with a mystery novel and licking all the chocolate from my favorite wheat-meal biscuits. But last night, after my sisters went to bed, the mysteries and the wheat meals were not their usual satisfying company. Merv, I called you because I can't seem to come up with a good enough answer for what's wrong with you. I like you.

MERV: Why?

SARA: Why?

MERV: It's a simple question.

SARA: You're a man who says he wants a grownup.

MERV: You call licking wheat-meal biscuits in bed grownup?

SARA: Maybe sometime you'd like to try it.

MERV: Sara, I think you need someone who's maybe a little more . . .

SARA: What?

MERV: Well, maybe a little less . . .

SARA: Merv, I don't think about us getting married, and I don't even need to get our children together, but sometime I'd really like to hear more about the concert of Europe.

MERV: From a post-industrial Zionist perspective?

SARA: If you're willing to debate it.

MERV: With you that could be difficult.

SARA: Grownups can be difficult.

MERV: But difficult can be engaging. Even surprising. I meant to tell you I had dinner last night at that tourist trap Simpson's in the Strand, and the bubble and squeak was rather good, actually.

SARA: Actually?

MERV: There are real possibilities in life, Sara, even for left-over meat and cabbage. And speaking of cabbage. The Rabbi of Dublin!

SARA: Go, go, go. *Gives him the Shiva statue.* Here, take this on your pilgrimage. It's the god Shiva.

MERV: The destroyer! I'm getting on a plane.

SARA: It'll ward off evil and bring you hope and rebirth.

MERV: You want me to worship pagan imagery?

SARA: I want to stir up your life a little, Mervyn Kantlowitz. Jesus Christ, why did your name have to be Mervyn? *She starts to hit him.* And you're a furrier!

MERV: Good-bye, Sara. *Kisses her.*

SARA: Let me know how you are.

MERV: You still have my shirt.

SARA: Give my regards to the Rabbi.

MERV: Today the rabbi of Dublin. Tomorrow the cantor of Cork. *Exits.*

TESS *enters in* GORGEOUS'S *original pink ensemble with full accessories and heels. She can hardly walk.*

SARA: What are you wearing?

TESS: Aunt Gorgeous says you can't accessorize enough. She said I should practice around the house. I think it's very "too-too."

SARA: I think it's maybe too "too-too" for the Lithuanian resistance.

TESS: I told Tom to go without me.

SARA: Thank you, honey.

TESS: I didn't make this decision for you. I made it for me. You have to have your own life.

SARA: Really, I can't have yours?

TESS: You wouldn't want mine. I don't even know what mine is. Mother, if I've never really been Jewish, and I'm not actually American anymore, and I'm not English or European, then who am I?

SARA: Tessie honey, as a child I was told that when your grandmother Rita was a girl, she was so smart, so competent, so beautiful and brave, that on the day the Cossacks came they were so impressed with her, they ran away.

TESS: I don't understand.

SARA: Everyone always told me, "Sadie, that Tessie of yours is just like Rita." So if Rita could make the Cossacks run away, you are smart enough, and brave enough, and certainly beautiful enough to find your place in the world.

TESS: Thank you, Mommy.

SARA: There are real possibilities in life, Tessie.

TESS: Mother!

SARA: Yes, honey.

TESS: If she was so beautiful, why did they run away?

SARA: I never understood that either. *Sits down on a chair.*

TESS: Can I ask you a few questions for this paper now? It's due tomorrow. *Turns on her tape recorder and kneels beside her mother.* Your name is? I know it's dumb, but we have to ask these things.

Pause.

SARA: My name is Sara Rosensweig. I am the daughter of Rita and Maury Rosensweig. I was born in Brooklyn, New York, August 23, 1937.

TESS: And when did you first sing?

SARA: I made my debut at La Scala at fourteen.

TESS: Mother!

SARA: I first sang at the Hanukah Festival at East Midwood Jewish Center. I played a candle.

TESS: And why did you become a Cliffe Clef?

SARA: Your great-grandfather thought I could be a singer.

TESS: Would you sing something now?

SARA: Honey, it's so early.

TESS: Please sing something. *Begins to sing:*

> Shine on, shine on, harvest moon
> Up in the sky.

SARA:

> I ain't had no loving since January, February, June or July.

"My name is Sara Rosensweig. I am the daughter of Rita and Maury Rosensweig." (Julie Dretzin, Jane Alexander) © 1992 Martha Swope

TESS: Do it, mother!
SARA *sings:*

Snow time ain't no time to stay outdoors and spoon.

TESS & SARA *sing:*

So shine on, shine on, harvest moon.

SARA *sings, touching her daughter's face:*

For me and my gal.

END